PERFECT PRESERVES

RECIPES FOR OVER 300 EASY-TO-MAKE PRESERVES

JOAN WILSON

PENGUIN BOOKS

PENGUIN BOOKS

Published by the Penguin Group
Penguin Books Ltd, 27 Wrights Lane, London W8 5TZ, England
Penguin Books USA Inc., 375 Hudson Street, New York, New York 10014, USA
Penguin Books Australia Ltd, Ringwood, Victoria, Australia
Penguin Books Canada Ltd, 10 Alcorn Avenue, Toronto, Ontario, Canada M4V 3B2
Penguin Books (NZ) Ltd, 182–190 Wairau Road, Auckland 10, New Zealand

Penguin Books Ltd, Registered Offices: Harmondsworth, Middlesex, England

First published in Australia by Viking O'Neil 1991
Published in Penguin Books 1996
10 9 8 7 6 5 4 3 2 1

Designed by Sandra Nobes
Cover photography by Alan Lindsay
Food preparation and styling by Helen Clucas
Typeset in Goudy Old Style by Bookset Pty Ltd, Melbourne
Printed in Australia by Australian Print Group, Maryborough, Victoria

CONTENTS

MEASUREMENTS & CONVERSIONS

Measurements used in this book are metric.
The standard measuring cup has a capacity of 250 ml.
All cup and spoon measures are taken at level.
The standard for measuring spoons is:

1 tablespoon	=	15 ml
1 teaspoon	=	5 ml

The recipes all give the amount of preserve produced. This is approximate; you may find the final jar is not completely full, or there may be a dribble that won't quite fit into the jars.

INTRODUCTION

With rich fruit flavours and jewel-like colours, home-made pre-serves are always firm favourites. There is infinite pleasure in surveying the jars of chunky marmalades and chutneys, colourful sauces and relishes and brilliant jellies and jams. The vivid green of mint and apple jelly is a joy to behold, and adds a piquant touch to a dish of succulent lamb.

The main attraction of home-made preserves is the essential quality of fruit flavour that is missing in commercially produced jams and jellies, which are overlaid with the taste of preservatives. For the most flavoursome results choose fruit that is at the height of its maturity, as fruits that are less ripe will never be quite as fruit-sweet.

A few pots of jam made in the fruit season – strawberry, raspberry, apple, quince, plum and apricot – will provide a welcome addition to the breakfast toast all through the winter. There is a ready wealth of taste sensations just waiting to be uncovered. During the flush of the vegetable crop, make pots of old-fashioned pickles and chutneys to add variety and interest to sausage or cold meat, chicken or hamburgers.

With the increase of 'pick your own' fruit or vegetables, home-made preserves have become a reality for everyone. There is no need to make a great production out of making jams or condiments. They can be made for pleasure in small batches, and it is far better to have a wide selection of a few jars of varied preserves than a lot of jars of just a few flavours.

Variety, they say, is the spice of life, so put that spice on your table top. Making a good preserve takes only a couple of hours of pleasant, rewarding work.

EQUIPMENT

Good equipment is vital if you want a good product.

1. THE PRESERVING PAN
   Use a large saucepan even if only a small quantity of jam is to be made; it must be large enough for the jam to boil briskly without boiling over. It should be made of thick, heavy metal so the jam will not burn. Copper, iron or brass pans should not be used for making chutneys, pickles, relishes or sauces, as the vinegar will react with the metal and produce a strange taste.

2. MEASURING EQUIPMENT
   Accurate kitchen scales, measuring jugs and graduated spoons are essential to make successful preserves.

3. LARGE WOODEN SPOON
   This should have a long handle. The fruit and sugar are boiled at a high temperature, and it is necessary to avoid your hands coming into contact with the extremely hot mixture.

4. SUGAR THERMOMETER
   This is very helpful in testing the jam. When jam reaches 105°C on the thermometer, it has reached setting point.

5. KNIFE
   A 'stay-sharp' knife (small size) is the best in my experience.

6. STRAINERS & SIEVES
   A colander and a range of large strainers or sieves are useful to remove the bag that contains seeds and/or peels from the jam, or to strain the mix when a jelly bag is not indicated.

7. JELLY BAG
   There are several methods of straining a fruit mixture.
   (a) From a specialist kitchen equipment store buy a conical jelly bag with attachments for hanging. This should be dampened before use.
   (b) Improvise a jelly bag by inverting a kitchen chair on the table and securely tying the corners of a cloth to the legs of the chair, leaving the cloth loose enough to dip in the

centre. On the inverted chair seat and under the cloth, place a large bowl. Pour the contents of the pan into the bag or cloth – not forcing the fruit through, or the jelly will be cloudy. With a tea towel or piece of greaseproof paper protect the mixture from dust or insects, and leave it for up to 12 hours so the liquid drips slowly through the cloth.

(c) For a small quantity of fruit mixture, put a piece of cloth in a colander or large strainer. Position over a large bowl and allow the liquid to drip through.

(d) If clarity of the liquid is not of prime importance, but time is of the utmost, the easiest and quickest way is to strain the mix into a bowl through a colander or a large strainer, pressing the fruit mixture with a wooden spoon to extract as much liquid as possible. Over another bowl place a strainer lined with a piece of cloth, and through this strain the liquid again to remove any remaining pulp.

8. JARS & BOTTLES

It is best to use larger jars for familiar, fast-moving jams, and smaller ones for unfamiliar flavours that may not be used as readily. Jars and bottles should never be used unless sterilised, to avoid contamination from micro-organisms or bacteria.

9. LIDS

Plastic or plastic-coated lids are necessary. Metal lids are liable to become corroded, which will give a metallic taste to the product. Alternatively use plastic covers.

10. COVERS

If jars are without lids, use jam covers – obtainable at supermarkets and newsagents. It is also a good idea to use these under plastic-coated lids that have had a fair amount of use.

11. JUG

A strong, wide, heatproof jug comes in handy when pouring the mixture.

12. FUNNELS

It is helpful to have plastic funnels to assist in pouring the hot mixtures into the jars.

13. LABELS

If the jars are not labelled and dated, then the question will be, 'What is it, and when was it made?'

STERILISING JARS & BOTTLES ·

The jars and bottles used to store preserves must be of glass (earthenware pots can be used to store mustards), without any cracks or chips. Wash the containers in detergent and rinse them well. Allow to drain. If you have a dishwasher, you can sterilise the cleaned jars or bottles using the rinse cycle and the hottest temperature, but no detergent. If you haven't a dishwasher, use one of the following methods.

1. STERILISING IN THE OVEN
   Wash the containers well in hot soapy water and rinse very thoroughly. Place them in a cold oven right way up on a board, but not allowing them to touch. Turn the oven on to very slow (120°C) and leave them there for 30 minutes. Remove from oven and cover with a clean cloth or clean paper.

2. STERILISING IN A PAN
   Wash the containers well in hot soapy water and rinse very thoroughly. Place a clean tea towel or such in the bottom of the pan. Lay the cleaned jars or bottles on their sides on the cloth in the pan. Cover completely with cold water, cover the pan and bring the water to the boil. Allow to boil for 20 minutes. Remove from the heat. With tongs, carefully remove the containers from the water and drain well. Stand them right way up on a wooden board, and cover with a clean cloth or clean paper.

Do not forget that the screw-top lids must also be well washed, rinsed and dried, and covered, in the same way as the jars and bottles.

Filling, Covering, Sealing & Storing

Preheat the jars (or bottles) to avoid cracking from the contact with the hot mixture. When the preserve is ready to put into jars remove the pan from the heat to prevent any further cooking. When pouring it into the jars, avoid hot splashes on your hand by using a wide, strong jug with a good lip. If this is not available, use a ladle.

The clean, sterilised hot jars should be standing on a layer of newspaper or a laminated or wooden surface. Fill jam, jelly, marmalade, chutney and relish jars right to the top – the preserve will shrink slightly when cooling. Put the jars to one side in a convenient place to cool. Cover them immediately with a clean cloth or a sheet of clean paper. As soon as the preserve is cool, cover the jars with circles of plastic wrap, greaseproof paper or jam covers purchased from the supermarket. Place the screw-tops in position and screw down, making sure that they are properly tightened to give a good seal.

Sauces are packed and corked while still hot, leaving a gap of about 2 cm below the cork or non-metallic screw top. Metallic tops should not be used in a recipe containing vinegar, as the vinegar will cause the metal to corrode.

Pickles do not need to be hot when being packed, as their preservation is dependent upon the concentration of vinegar. They should have a 1 cm to 2 cm gap below the rim. Metallic tops should not be used for pickles.

Chutneys and relishes can dry out and shrink if they are not covered with cellophane or a layer of paraffin wax under the non-metallic lids.

After the jars of preserves are sealed, wipe them thoroughly to remove any sugar or material that could cause mould to form. Dry them and attach labels. On these write the name of the preserve and the date. Light has an adverse effect on stored preserves, causing them to deteriorate, so store them in a cool, airy, dry, dark place. If you live in a wet, humid climate, a refrigerator is the best place to store preserves, and is also the place to keep an opened jar.

MAKING PERFECT JAM, JELLY & MARMALADE

Good quality fruit is the prime ingredient for making good quality jam. It should be used as soon as possible after it has been picked. All edible fruits may be used, and also some vegetables such as marrow and tomatoes.

Jam is a mixture of fruit and sugar used in proportions that allow jellying of the mixture after the required cooking time. Conserve is jam in which the fruit is whole or is in big pieces. Good jam has a clear flavour, an even texture and a firm set. It must not be too stiff, but should hold its shape on a spoon. It should be of good colour, with the fruit evenly distributed.

Three things are needed to make jam set:

- **sugar**
- **acid**
- **pectin**.

Some fruits are naturally low in acid and pectin, and lemon juice is included in these recipes to compensate for this. Don't try to use commercial lemon squeeze 'juice' – it won't work. You must add freshly squeezed lemon juice to ensure the jam will set.

Sugar is the preservative in jam making, and enough must be used to prevent the formation of mould or fermentation. White crystal-lised table sugar is used in jam making, though loaf and castor will give the same result, the only difference being that castor sugar can dissolve faster, but is dearer. (In chutneys, sauces, pickles and relishes, white or brown sugar is used, with brown sugar giving a richer flavour and colour.)

Warming of the sugar before adding to the pan is largely a matter of choice. Some claim that this will help achieve clarity by ensuring the sugar dissolves faster, allowing the jam or jelly to reach the jellying point more quickly. To warm sugar, turn the oven on to slow heat (130°C). Spread the sugar, no more than 3 cm deep, in a baking dish and place in the oven for no more than 10 minutes, stirring occasionally to distribute the heat. Do not allow it to overheat or become browned.

COOKING PROCEDURES FOR JAM

There are two basic methods of making jam. Both produce good jams.

METHOD 1
Fruit and water are boiled together until soft pulp results. Sugar is then added until testing shows that the setting point has been reached. The setting point should generally be reached within 20 minutes. If you cook for much longer the fruit flavour of the jam will be impaired.

METHOD 2
Fruit is cut up, sprinkled with sugar and left to stand overnight so that the juices are drawn from the fruit to make a liquid. The mixture is then boiled until the setting point is reached, again within about 20 minutes.

THE AMOUNT OF SUGAR TO USE

Sugar is needed to make the jam keep, and sufficient must be used to prevent fermentation, or the formation of mould. Too much sugar will make the jam go syrupy, preventing a good set. Not enough sugar will allow the jam to deteriorate and also prevent setting.

The proportion of sugar needed is generally between 750 g and 1 kg of sugar to each kg of prepared fruit. Every 1 kg of sugar used should produce about 1.75 kg of jam, jelly or marmalade. When measuring fruit to determine the quantity of sugar required in recipes in this book, measure in cups.

PECTIN CONTENT OF FRUITS

The following table identifies fruit according to its pectin content. The amount of sugar, water and lemon juice recommended refers to 1 kg of fruit weighed after peeling, etc.

HIGH SETTING QUALITY

The pectin in these fruits can set a high amount of sugar. A fair amount of water will be needed, or the jam will be too stiff.

FRUIT (1 kg)	WATER NEEDED	SUGAR	LEMON JUICE
apples (green)	1 cup	1 kg	—
blackcurrants	2–3 cups	1.1 kg	—
damsons	1–2 cups	1.1 kg	—
gooseberries (green)	1–2 cups	1.1 kg	—
quinces	1–2 cups	1.1 kg	2 tablespoons

REASONABLE SETTING QUALITY

As these fruits are juicy, they need little or no water. When no added water is indicated, mash the fruit in the pan to extract some of the juice, then simmer gently until a smooth purée is obtained.

FRUIT (1 kg)	WATER NEEDED	SUGAR	LEMON JUICE
blueberries	—	1 kg	—
cooking cherries (stoned)	4–6 tablespoons	800 g	—
cooking cherries (unstoned)	4–6 tablespoons	1 kg	—
gooseberries (ripe)	—	1 kg	—
greengages	—	1 kg	—
loganberries	—	1 kg	—
passionfruit	—	1 kg	—
plums	—	1 kg	—
raspberries	—	1 kg	—
rhubarb	—	1 kg	—

POOR SETTING QUALITY
Being deficient in pectin, these fruits need lemon juice or red-currant juice for a good set. If no added water is indicated mash the fruit in the pan to extract the juice.

FRUIT (1 kg)	WATER NEEDED	SUGAR	LEMON JUICE
apricots (fresh)	4 tablespoons	1 kg	juice of 2 large lemons
apricots (dried)	7 cups	2.75 kg	juice of 4–6 large lemons
blackberries	—	1 kg	juice of 1 lemon
cherries, dessert (stoned)	—	800 g	juice of 2 lemons
cherries, dessert (unstoned)	—	1 kg	juice of 2 lemons
figs (fresh)	4 tablespoons	1 kg	juice of 2 large lemons
figs (dried)	7 cups	2.75 kg	juice of 4–6 large lemons
guavas	6 tablespoons	1 kg	juice of 1 lemon
lychees	—	1 kg	juice of 2 lemons
mangoes	6 tablespoons	1 kg	juice of 1 lemon
melons	—	1 kg	juice of 4 lemons
peaches	4 tablespoons	1 kg	juice of 2 large lemons
pineapples	—	1 kg	juice of 2 lemons
strawberries	—	800 g	juice of 2 lemons
tomatoes	—	1 kg	juice of 2 lemons

TO TEST FOR PECTIN CONTENT

The amount of pectin in fruit can be estimated quite accurately. The pectin is extracted by simmering fruit in a little water until it is soft. If the fruit is a 'poor setter' (see table on page 9) add 2 tablespoons of fresh lemon juice or ½ teaspoon of citric acid or tartaric acid to each 1.75 kg of fruit.

To test for pectin, put 1 teaspoon of juice from the pan into a small tumbler. Let it stand until cold. Add 3 tablespoons of methylated spirit and shake gently. Leave for 1 minute. The amount of pectin in the juice will be indicated by the clots or lumps of a jelly-like substance that appear:

- a large lump indicates that plenty of pectin is present and up to 3 cups of sugar may be added to each 500 g of fruit
- 2 or 3 less firm clots indicate moderate pectin content and 2 cups of sugar may be added to each 500 g of fruit
- lots of small clots indicate little pectin and the jam is unlikely to set unless pectin stock or another high-pectin fruit is added.

TO MAKE PECTIN STOCK

Pectin stock is usually made from cooking apples. Chop these up but do not peel or core. Gooseberries or red currants may also be used. Put these in the pan and mash a little with a potato masher. It is not necessary to top or tail them, but do be sure to wash them first.

Put 1 kg of fruit and 2½ cups of water in a pan. Bring slowly to the boil, then simmer for about 30 minutes until the fruit is very soft. Test for pectin. If a firm clot does not appear, simmer for a little longer, until a firm clot forms when tested. Strain through a jelly bag. Bring the strained juice to the boil and then pour it into hot, sterilised jars. Use within 4 months.

TO TEST FOR SETTING

It will be necessary to test the jam mixture to make certain that the setting point has been reached. Test early for setting point; always turn off the heat and carefully remove the pan from the stove before testing, otherwise the jam may become overcooked.

You will be warned that the jam has nearly reached setting point when rapid frothing ceases and it makes heavy, plopping noises, or you can rely on a jam thermometer. Jam has reached setting point when it is 105°C.

A setting test may be done on a saucer or a wooden spoon. Put a saucer in the freezer and leave it until it becomes cold. Take it from the freezer and on it place a little jam and allow this to cool. If the setting point has been reached a skin will form that will wrinkle when it is pushed with the finger. The jam is now ready to be put into jars.

If using the spoon test, stir the jam with the wooden spoon, take the spoon from the jam and twist it around until the jam on it has cooled. If setting point has been reached, this jam will have thickened, drops will run together and form large flakes that adhere to the spoon. If the jam is still runny, it is not yet ready, so continue to boil until the setting point is reached.

When you are sure the jam has reached setting point, remove any scum from the top of the mixture with a long-handled spoon. It may be possible to disperse the scum if it is stirred carefully and slowly with a strong wide spatula (about 8 cm wide) or a strong metal egg-slice. For this purpose I have a strong straight-edged trowel that has proved to be invaluable. They are obtainable from hardware shops or from specialist kitchen equipment suppliers.

COMMON PROBLEMS

1. FAILURE TO SET

This can be caused by using incorrect proportions of sugar, pectin and acid. It may also be caused by insufficient cooking, or by not having reached the setting point. If the jam has set only lightly, the jars may be put in a heated oven that has been turned off. This little extra heat may sometimes be enough to complete the jellying process. If the jam is runny after bottling, empty it back into a pan, reheat it carefully, then retest it for setting. The jars will need to be washed and sterilised again before they are refilled.

2. HARD OR CHEWY

This is caused by overcooking, and going past the setting point. It cannot be solved.

3. MOULD ON TOP

This may be caused by three things:
- using insufficient sugar
- inadequate cooking
- dampness in covering or storing.

If there is mould on the jam, and it is not too deep, carefully scoop the mould away and also take 10 cm off the top of the jam. The rest is edible.

4. SUGARY ON TOP

This is due to one or all three reasons:
- too much sugar used
- stored for too long
- sugar inadequately dissolved in cooking.

It is best to take off the top layer of sugar and use the rest of the jam quickly. The batch could be reheated and repacked into clean, sterilised jars, but the keeping quality of the jam will be affected.

5. FERMENTATION

The preserve will taste slightly acidic and there will be bubbles in it. The causes of fermentation are as follows:
- fruit starting to deteriorate
- poorly cleaned jars or lids
- poor covering of jars
- warm storage conditions.

Jam that has fermented is like bad wine. Dispose of it.

TWELVE GOLDEN RULES

1. Avoid boiling the jam too quickly to soften the fruit, or too slowly after the sugar has been dissolved.

2. Avoid adding the sugar too early when cooking fruit that has tough skin. Once the sugar has been added, the skin will not soften any further.

3. Avoid using over-ripe fruit. Mature fruit needs extra cooking.

4. Avoid using any fruit that has brown rot, or any disease.

5. Avoid using any damaged or bruised pieces of fruit.

6. Avoid using fruit that has not been washed.

7. Avoid using too much sugar. It will make the jam go syrupy, and will prevent a good set.

8. Avoid using too little sugar. Too little sugar will also make a badly set jam, and will allow the jam to deteriorate.

9. Avoid allowing the jam to burn. Stir frequently in the initial stages, when some fruits are inclined to burn easily.

10. Avoid using high heat when adding the sugar. When adding the sugar, stir over a low heat until it is dissolved completely. This prevents the sugar from crystallising during keeping.

11. Avoid the use of a pan that is too small, as jam boils up very quickly.

12. Avoid trying to make too much at one time. It is best to make jam in lots of 1.5 kg or less, as the setting point is then reached quickly, and the flavour and colour of the fruit is retained.

GLOSSARY

ALCOHOL This optional extra gives a particular flavour, and can be added to preserves according to personal taste. In the case of liqueurs, those flavoured with a particular fruit have an obvious affinity with the fruit from which they are made. This gives an idea as to which liqueur suits a particular preserve.

brandy A spirit that may be added, with discretion, to any jam. It goes well with fruits such as apricots and peaches, and gives a special flavouring to marmalades.

Calvados A French brandy made from apples, and first produced in Calvados in Normandy.

Cointreau An orange-flavoured liqueur.

gin A colourless liquor made by distilling rye, barley or other grain, and flavoured with juniper berries. I rarely use gin, except in the making of some fruit liqueurs.

grenadine A thick, sweet syrup, bright red in colour, made from pomegranates or red currants and used as a non-alcoholic flavouring.

kirsch Use in cherry or pineapple conserve.

port May be added, with discretion, to any jam.

rum Made from fermented molasses or sugar cane and can be used in many preserves. It goes well with apples, mixed berries, oranges and plums. Generally, I use a dark, underproof rum, although white rum is best for fruit liqueurs.

vodka Fermented from a mash of rye, wheat or potatoes, this is a colourless liquor that I use mostly in fruit liqueurs.

whisky Use a good-quality Scotch whisky. Made by distilling fermented malted barley, this spirit makes an excellent flavouring for marmalades.

wine If a white wine is required, I use a moselle; in recipes that call for red wine, any red wine will do.

APPLES

cooking These are the best apples to use in making conserve, jam or jelly, as when green these contain the most pectin, which is so necessary for a good set. Do not waste time preserve making with eating apples.

windfalls These are apples that have either fallen from the tree or have been blown off by the wind. They are a good buy and are perfect for cooking, as unripe apples have plenty of acid and give extra flavour. Windfalls are particularly good for making jelly.

ALLSPICE Available either whole or ground, allspice is an aromatic berry from the tropical American pimenta tree. It is called allspice after its supposed flavour of a mixture of nutmeg, cinnamon and cloves.

BLUEBERRY This small berry is now readily available throughout the summer.

CAPE GOOSEBERRY This plant is not a true gooseberry; it is related to the tomato. It grows wild in the USA, Mexico, Peru and Chile. It is now cultivated in Australia for its fruit, which can be eaten either raw or made into jam. The fruit is a globular, yellow berry with a paper-like covering. The matured fruit has a pale brown husk that is easily removed.

CARDAMOM A member of the ginger family. This aromatic Asian spice is available as seeds, pods or in powder form. The powdered cardamom has a much more floury flavour than the whole seeds. Cardamom is particularly suited to using in relishes.

CAYENNE PEPPER A sweet, pungent, very hot, ground red pepper.

CHILLI The pod of a small pepper or capsicum. It may be dried and ground to a powder. Fresh chilli should be used with care. Since the seeds are extremly hot, they may be removed and discarded if preferred.

CHOKO A pear-shaped, pale-green fruit of a climbing vine, prepared as a vegetable in the same manner as the marrow. Chokoes thrive in hot weather and are grown mainly in sub-tropical areas. In more temperate zones they are available in spring and summer.

CINNAMON Cinnamon is a spice available in stick or ground form. The sticks are dried, aromatic pieces of bark taken from the tropical tree.

CITRIC ACID A colourless, translucent, crystalline acid mainly derived from lemon, lime and pineapple juices. Used as a flavouring or as an aid in jam setting.

CLOVES The unopened aromatic buds of an east Indian tree that are used, whole or ground, as a spice.

CRABAPPLE A deciduous small tree that is grown both for the beauty of its spring blossom and for the fruit, which is used for jam and jelly making. Crabapples are particularly high in pectin.

CUMIN The aromatic seeds of the cumin plant, used as a spice.

CUMQUAT Or kumquat. A small, edible, orange-like fruit having acid pulp and a thin, edible rind. It is usually home-grown and ripens in late spring and summer. It has a distinctive flavour that is popular in jams and marmalades.

DAMSON An oval, bluish-black, juicy plum, mainly used for jam. It comes into season in summer and is available from most fruit markets.

ELDERBERRY The small, black, edible fruit of the elder bush. Elderberries are well worth growing. Available in summer from most fruit markets.

FEIJOA A native of Brazil, the feijoa is grown as an ornamental shrub in Australia and is very common. Its fruit has a flavour similar to that of the guava. The fruit is in season for a short time in autumn.

FULL ROLLING BOIL *see* **HARD BOIL**

GARAM MASALA A mixture of spices used in curries. It usually includes cardamom, clove, cumin and pepper. However, there are many versions of garam masala, and most cooks use their own favourite combinations of spices.

GINGER

crystallised Peeled root ginger that is crystallised in sugar.

ground Dried and powdered root ginger.

preserved Peeled root ginger preserved in syrup.

root The pungent aromatic rootstock of the ginger plant. Sometimes referred to as green ginger.

GREENGAGE A variety of plum with sweet flesh and yellowish-green skin. Available from most fruit markets in summer.

GUAVA A pear-shaped tropical fruit with a yellow rind and pink flesh. Guavas are grown commercially in northern Australia. They are best known for their jelly. In temperate zones the fruit ripens in summer. It is commercially available throughout the year as it is kept in cool storage.

HARD BOIL Or to bring to a *full rolling boil* is to heat until boiling and to keep heating while the mixture is seething.

JAPONICA A small, quince-like fruit, also known as the flowering quince, which is used in jellies. It ripens in early summer, and is not available commercially.

LOGANBERRY A dark red berry fruit. It is basically a cross between a blackberry and a raspberry. Available commercially in season – autumn.

LOQUAT A smallish, yellow, pear-shaped fruit that is principally used to make jams, jellies and sauces. It is in season from November to February (late spring and summer) and is available commercially at this time.

MACADAMIA NUTS These are the edible, sweet, butter-flavoured, nut-like seeds of the macadamia tree, native to eastern Australia. These nuts can be substituted for walnuts in most recipes.

MACE An aromatic spice made from the dried, waxy covering that partly encloses the nutmeg kernel.

MIXED PEEL Available commercially, this is a mixture of a variety of crystallised citrus peels.

MIXED SPICE This is a blend of various ground spices, including allspice, cinnamon and nutmeg, and is used as a flavouring. Commercially available from supermarkets.

MUSTARD SEEDS The seeds of various species of the mustard plant. The white and the yellow seeds are aromatic, and the brown and the black are pungent.

NUTMEG A hard, aromatic, round seed used as a spice in powdered form or else freshly grated.

ORANGE, SEVILLE Suitable only for jam making. This rather tart orange makes very good marmalade.

PECTIN Found in certain fruits and vegetables. When heated with sugar it forms a gel and helps jam, jelly or marmalade to set. If there is not enough natural pectin present in the fruit, a commercial pectin preparation such as Jamsetta will help.

PECTIN STOCK This is usually prepared from cooking apples, red currants or gooseberries. It can be a commercial product or homemade (see p. 10), and is used in jam making to add to varieties of fruit that are in themselves low in pectin.

PEPPERS Known also as capsicum, these are mild, sweet and red or green. Regarded as one of the richest natural sources of vitamin C, they are also sources of vitamins A and B.

PERSIMMON An orange-red tropical fruit that is edible only when ripe. Commercially available in summer.

PICKLING ONION Small onion that is peeled and used for pickling in vinegar and spices.

PICKLING SPICE A ground mixture of spices, available from supermarkets.

PICKLING SPICES A mixture of whole spices for pickling, available from supermarkets. If pickling spices are ground, the colour of the end product is changed (for instance, ground spices will cloud any vinegar), although this may be a feature of the recipe. If whole spices are used, they can be put in a muslin bag and removed. You can make up your own mixture (e.g. cloves, crushed dried chillies, allspice, garlic, mustard seeds, cinnamon stick, root ginger, cardamom, etc.).

PIMENTO The mild, ripe, red fruit of sweet peppers.

PITH The white, fibrous tissue between the rind and the pulp in citrus fruits.

QUINCE An aromatic, many-seeded fruit, rich in pectin, used extensively in jam and jelly making. Commercially available in autumn.

RIND The skin or surface layer of fruits, as distinct from the pith, which comes between the rind and the pulp.

ROSE PETALS   Use petals of a fragrant red rose and cut off any white ends before using.

ROWANBERRY The small, red, berry-like fruit of the rowan tree, which is a Scandinavian variety of the mountain ash. Makes an excellent jelly. This fruit is not readily available commercially. Ripens in summer.

SUGAR The preservative used in making jams is sugar. It must be added to the jam and stirred in without boiling, until dissolved, after which the jam is brought to the boil very quickly and boiled as rapidly as possible. Though sugar made in Australia is of a very high quality, a lower grade is creeping in on supermarket shelves – a cheaper brand of sugar that tends to cause more scum during this boiling process. Different types of sugar can be used.

white granulated Excellent for jam and for preserves where the colour of the fruit or the vegetable should remain unchanged.

brown sugar Generally gives a richer flavour and colour to chutneys, sauces, pickles and relishes. It is slightly darker than raw sugar, which must not be used in preserve making.

soft brown sugar Usually contains less molasses, is more quickly dissolved and gives a different texture to that obtained when either brown or white sugar is used.

TAMARILLO A red, fleshy fruit about the size of a passionfruit, with black seeds. The skin is astringent and should be peeled off. Drop the fruit into hot water, stand for 3 or 4 minutes, then peel off the skin with a sharp knife. Tamarillos are grown in Australian gardens but those available in shops are mostly imported from New Zealand. They are often used in jams.

TARTARIC ACID Used in making sweets and preserves to prevent the sugar from crystallising. Sometimes available in specialty health-food stores. It must be kept in an airtight container.

TURMERIC A ground, dried, brilliant yellow root that has a bitter flavour. It is used in pickles, chutneys and mustards and is an essential ingredient in curry powder. It is used mainly as a colouring.

VINEGAR This is a sour by-product of fermentation that has gone beyond the alcohol stage, and is used as a condiment and preservative. There are many varieties.

cider Made from apples.

distilled White vinegar that has a higher acetic acid content, and is the best for preserving.

malt Made from barley.

white White, brown or red vinegars are made from grapes.

wine Made from a better quality grape than the other vinegars. It has not gone quite as far in the fermentation process and is not as sharp or sour as ordinary white vinegar. It is a higher-quality vinegar and is more expensive.

JAMS

Before starting, read Making Perfect Jam, Jelly & Marmalade on pp. 6–13, particularly the section Cooking Procedures for Jam on p. 7. Other useful tips can be found in the boxes at the base of many pages in this book.

ALMOND AND APRICOT JAM

Makes 5 × 350 ml jars

---

500 g dried apricots
5 cups water
6 cups sugar
½ cup blanched almonds
½ teaspoon almond essence

Cut apricots into pieces, and soak in water overnight in a non-metallic bowl. Next day, sterilise the jars, then drain the water into a heavy based pan, add the sugar and stir over low heat until dissolved. Add the apricots. Simmer until thickened – this jam does not require a pectin test. Add almonds and essence. Pour into hot jars, cover while cooling and seal when cool.

APPLE JAM

Makes 7 × 350 ml jars

1.5 kg cooking apples
2⅓ cups water
juice of 2 lemons
1.5 kg sugar

First sterilise the jars. Peel, core and slice the apples, and place in pan with the water and the lemon juice. Simmer until tender. Add the sugar, stirring until it is dissolved. Bring to the boil. Continue boiling until setting point is reached. Pour into hot jars. Cover until cool, then seal.

APPLE AND APRICOT JAM

Makes 6 × 350 ml jars

---

1 kg cooking apples
1 kg apricots
2½ cups water
sugar

Sterilise the jars. Peel, core and slice apples. Cut apricots in half and remove stones. Put fruit and water in a heavy based pan and simmer until fruit is pulpy. Measure pulp and return to pan. Add ¾ cup of sugar to each cup of pulp. Stir over low heat until sugar dissolves, then boil until setting point is reached. Pour into hot jars, cover until cold and then seal.

APPLE AND BLACKBERRY JAM

Makes 7 × 350 ml jars

---

1 kg cooking apples
⅔ cup water
1 kg blackberries
2 kg sugar

Sterilise the jars. Peel, core and chop apples. Put in a heavy based pan with water. Cook gently until the apples are just soft, then add the blackberries. Simmer until the fruit is soft, stir in the sugar until it dissolves, then boil rapidly until setting point is reached. Pour into hot jars. Cover until cold, then seal.

APPLE AND BLACKCURRANT JAM

Makes 9 × 350 ml jars

---

500 g cooking apples
2½ cups water
1 kg blackcurrants
6 cups sugar

First sterilise the jars. Peel, core and chop apples. Put in a heavy based pan with water. Cook gently until the fruit is soft. Add blackcurrants and bring to the boil. Simmer until soft and pulpy. Stir in sugar until it is dissolved. Boil rapidly to setting point, stirring occasionally. Pour into hot jars and cover until cool, then seal.

APPLE AND BLUEBERRY JAM

Makes 4 × 350 ml jars

---

3 cups peeled, cored and finely sliced
  cooking apples
3 cups blueberries
¼ cup lemon juice
4 cups sugar

Sterilise the jars. Put apples, blueberries and lemon juice in a heavy based pan and boil until fruit is soft. Stir in the sugar until dissolved. Bring back to boil, and continue boiling briskly until the setting point is reached. Pack into hot jars, cover until cool and seal.

APPLE AND CINNAMON JAM

Makes 7 × 350 ml jars

1.5 kg cooking apples
juice of 2 lemons
1 teaspoon ground cinnamon
2⅓ cups water
1.5 kg sugar

First sterilise the jars. Peel, core and slice apples. Place the apples, lemon juice, cinnamon and water in a heavy pan, and simmer until the fruit is tender. Add sugar, stirring until dissolved. Boil briskly until setting point is reached. Pour into hot jars. Cover until cool, then seal.

APPLE AND GINGER JAM

Makes 7 × 350 ml jars

1.5 kg cooking apples
25 g root ginger, peeled
2⅓ cups water
juice and grated rind of 2 lemons
1.5 kg sugar
125 g crystallised ginger

Sterilise the jars. Peel, core and slice apples. Bruise root ginger and place in muslin bag with apple peel and cores. Secure the bag and put in pan with apples, water, lemon juice and rind. Simmer until tender; remove bag. Add sugar and chopped crystallised ginger. Stir until sugar is dissolved. Boil to setting point. Pour into hot jars and cover. Seal when cool.

APPLE AND FIG JAM

Makes 6 × 350 ml jars

---

1 kg green or purple figs
250 g cooking apples
juice and finely grated rind of 2 lemons
5 cups sugar

Sterilise the jars. Top the figs to remove stem, then halve or quarter, as desired. Peel, core and slice the apples, and place them in a heavy pan with the figs, lemon juice and rind. Cook gently until fruit is soft. Stir in the sugar until dissolved. Boil until setting point is reached. Cool a little. Pour into hot jars and cover. Seal when cold.

APPLE AND GOOSEBERRY JAM

Makes 7 × 350 ml jars

---

3 cooking apples
water
500 g gooseberries
1 tablespoon lemon juice
3 cups sugar

First sterilise the jars. Wash apples, chop roughly and put in pan with just enough water to cover. Bring to boil and simmer for 30 minutes. Strain through jelly bag. Place the apple liquid, crushed gooseberries, lemon juice and sugar in a large, heavy pan. Heat gently and stir until sugar is dissolved, then boil rapidly until setting point is reached. Pack in hot jars, cover until cool, then seal.

APPLE AND LEMON JAM

Makes 7 × 350 ml jars

---

6 lemons
3 kg cooking apples
12 cups water
juice of 2 lemons
4.5 kg sugar

Slice the 6 lemons very thinly and soak in water in a non-metallic bowl, covered, overnight. Next morning, sterilise the jars, then peel, core and slice the apples, and place in a heavy pan with the lemons and 12 cups of water. Boil for 1 hour, add lemon juice, then stir in sugar until dissolved. Boil again rapidly for 1 hour, until setting point is reached. Pack in hot jars, cover until cool and seal.

APPLE AND LOGANBERRY JAM

Makes 12 × 350 ml jars

---

1 kg cooking apples
2 kg loganberries
12 cups sugar

First sterilise the jars. Peel, core and slice apples. Put in a large, heavy pan with the loganberries. Cook over low heat, stirring frequently until the fruit is soft. Stir in the sugar until dissolved. Increase heat. Bring to a brisk boil until setting point is reached. Skim foam off the surface before pouring into hot jars. Cover until cool, then seal and store.

APPLE AND MARROW JAM

Makes 7 × 350 ml jars

1.5 kg cooking apples
1.5 kg marrow
1.5 kg sugar
juice and grated rind of 2 lemons

Peel, core and slice apples. Peel marrow, remove seeds and cut in 2.5-cm cubes. Put marrow in layers with apple and sugar in a non-metallic bowl. Cover bowl and leave overnight. Next day, sterilise the jars, then transfer marrow, apple and sugar to a heavy based pan. Add lemon juice and rind and simmer, stirring, until the sugar dissolves. Boil until the marrow is clear and the setting point is reached. Pour into hot jars, cover until cool, then seal.

APPLE AND PASSIONFRUIT JAM

Makes 7 × 350 ml jars

1.5 kg cooking apples
juice of 2 lemons
2 cups water
24 passionfruit
1.5 kg sugar

First sterilise the jars. Peel, core and slice apples. Put in a pan with lemon juice, water and pulp from the passionfruit. Simmer until the fruit is tender. Stir in the sugar until it dissolves, then boil rapidly until setting point is reached. Pour into hot jars, cover, cool, and seal.

APPLE AND PEAR JAM

Makes 8 × 350 ml jars

2.5 kg cooking pears
1 kg cooking apples
2.5-cm piece peeled root ginger
juice and rind of 3 lemons
3½ cups water
3 kg sugar

Sterilise the jars. Peel, core and quarter pears. Peel, core and slice apples. Crush ginger. In a muslin bag tie the lemon rind, cores, peels and crushed ginger. Put fruit, water and bag in a heavy based pan. Simmer until fruit is soft. Remove bag. Stir in sugar until dissolved. Add lemon juice. Boil until setting point is reached. Pour into hot jars. Cover until cool, then seal.

APPLE AND PLUM JAM

Makes 8 × 350 ml jars

750 g peeled, cored and sliced cooking
    apples
750 g plums, halved and pitted
1¼ cups water
1 tablespoon lemon juice
5 cups sugar

First sterilise the jars. Put apples, plums, water and lemon juice in a heavy based pan. Bring to a quick boil. Reduce heat, and cook until the fruit is soft. Stir in the sugar until it is dissolved. Bring back to brisk boil until setting point is reached. Remove from heat and skim foam from surface. Pour into hot jars. Cover, cool, then seal.

APPLE AND PINEAPPLE JAM

Makes 15 × 350 ml jars

juice of 3 lemons
1.5 kg chopped fresh pineapple flesh
500 g peeled, cored and sliced cooking
    apples
2½ cups water
6 cups sugar

Sterilise the jars. Put lemon juice, pineapple, apple and water in a heavy pan and bring to boil. Reduce heat. Simmer until the pineapple is tender. Stir in sugar until dissolved. Boil briskly without stirring, until setting point is reached. Stand, off the heat, for 5 minutes before pouring into hot jars. Cover until cool, then seal.

APPLE AND QUINCE JAM

Makes 6 × 350 ml jars

1 kg windfall apples
1 kg quinces
water
sugar

Sterilise the jars. Wash fruit. Cut away any bad pieces. Chop roughly. Put in deep pan. Cover with water. Simmer gently, until fruit pulps. Strain through sieve to remove cores, pips and peel. Measure pulp, put in a heavy based pan and bring to boil. Stir in 1 cup of sugar to each cup of pulp. Boil to the setting point. Pack in hot jars, cover until cool and then seal.

APPLE AND RASPBERRY JAM

Makes 9 × 350 ml jars

---

1 kg cooking apples
1 kg raspberries
water
3 tablespoons lemon juice
1 kg sugar

First sterilise the jars. Peel, core and slice apples. Place in a heavy pan with the raspberries and a little water, and heat gently. Stir a little until the mixture boils. Stir in the lemon juice, then the sugar until it dissolves. Boil rapidly until setting point is reached. Pour into hot jars. Cover until cool, then seal.

APPLE AND RED-CURRANT JAM

Makes 6 × 350 ml jars

---

1 kg cooking apples
2 kg red currants
3 kg sugar

Sterilise the jars. Peel, core and slice apples, and place in a pan with the red currants. Simmer the fruit very gently until the juice runs well. Warm sugar in a low oven (about 130°C). Add the warmed sugar to the pan and stir well to dissolve. Boil briskly until setting point is reached. Remove from heat. Pour into hot jars. Cover until cool, then seal.

APPLE AND STRAWBERRY JAM

Makes 6 × 350 ml jars

---

500 g cooking apples
1 kg strawberries
juice of 2 lemons
1.5 kg sugar

Sterilise the jars. Peel, core and slice apples. Hull the strawberries. Place together in a heavy based pan. Simmer until fruit is soft. Add lemon juice. Gently stir in the sugar until it is dissolved. Boil briskly until setting point is reached, then pour into hot jars. Cover until cool, then seal.

APRICOT JAM

Makes 6 × 350 ml jars

---

1 kg apricots
1 kg sugar
1 cup water

Sterilise the jars. Wash, stone and slice apricots. In a heavy pan dissolve sugar in water over a low heat. Bring to boil for 2 or 3 minutes. Add apricots to syrup. Boil for 30–35 minutes, stirring jam occasionally to prevent sticking. Test for setting. Pack, cover until cool and seal.

SPECIAL APRICOT JAM

Makes 6 × 350 ml jars

1 kg apricots
1 kg sugar
1 cup water

First sterilise the jars. Wash, stone and halve apricots. Extract 4–6 kernels from the stones and blanch them in boiling water. After 5–10 minutes test a kernel. If the skin rubs off they are ready for use. Remove skins and slice. Over a low heat dissolve sugar in water in a heavy pan. Boil for 2 or 3 minutes. Add sliced kernels and apricots to this syrup. Stir occasionally while mixture boils for 30–35 minutes. Test for setting point. When ready pour into hot jars, cover until cool, then seal.

APRICOT AND BRANDY JAM

Makes 6 × 350 ml jars

1.5 kg apricots
2 cups cold water
juice of 2 lemons
6 cups sugar
¾ cup brandy

Sterilise the jars. Halve apricots. Remove stones. Remove kernels from one-third of the stones. Blanch kernels in some boiling water. After 5–10 minutes test a kernel. If the skin rubs off they are ready. Remove skins and slice. Put the apricots, kernels, water and lemon juice in a heavy pan. Simmer until the fruit is tender, and test for pectin (see p. 10). When satisfactory, stir in sugar until dissolved. Boil rapidly to setting point. Stir in brandy. Pack in hot jars, cover until cool and seal.

DRIED APRICOT AND PEACH JAM

Makes 4 × 350 ml jars

225 g dried apricots
3 cups water
750 g frozen peaches in syrup or
　2 × 425 g cans peaches in syrup
3 tablespoons lemon juice
4½ cups sugar

Place apricots in a non-metallic bowl. Add the water, cover and leave overnight. Stand peaches in a dish to thaw. Next day, sterilise the jars, then transfer apricots and water to a heavy based pan, bring to boil and simmer gently until soft. Add the peaches and lemon juice, and simmer until pulpy. Stir in the sugar until dissolved. Boil rapidly until setting point is reached. Pour into hot jars. Cover until cool and seal.

DON'T FORGET TO LABEL AND DATE YOUR PRESERVES

DRIED APRICOT AND PINEAPPLE JAM

Makes 4 × 350 ml jars

---

225 g dried apricots
2½ cups water
1 × 454 g can crushed pineapple
3½ cups sugar

Soak apricots in the water in a non-metallic bowl overnight. Next day, sterilise the jars, then transfer fruit and water to a heavy pan, bring to the boil and simmer gently until tender. Add crushed pineapple and sugar, and stir constantly until sugar dissolves. Bring to full rolling boil. Continue boiling rapidly to setting point. Pack in hot jars, cover until cool, then seal.

DRIED APRICOT, PINE-APPLE AND GINGER JAM

Makes 3 × 350 ml jars

---

225 g dried apricots
2½ cups water
1 × 454 g can crushed pineapple
250 g crystallised ginger, sliced
3½ cups sugar

Put dried apricots and water in a non-metallic bowl and soak overnight. Next day, sterilise the jars, then transfer apricots and water to a heavy based pan and bring mixture to the boil. Simmer gently until apricots are tender. Add pineapple and ginger. Stir in sugar until dissolved. Bring to full rolling boil and boil to setting point. Pack in hot jars, cover, cool, and seal.

THREE-MINUTE BERRY JAM

Makes 2 × 350 ml jars

2½ cups berries (loganberries,
*   raspberries, or boysenberries)*
2¼ cups sugar

Sterilise the jars. Place the berries and sugar in a heavy pan and heat gently, stirring frequently until the sugar has been dissolved. Then boil briskly for 3 minutes. Very ripe fruit will take a further 1 minute. Pour into hot jars, cover until cool and seal. Jam will appear lightly set at first, but will thicken after a few days.

BLACKBERRY JAM

Makes 5 × 300 ml jars

---

1 kg blackberries
juice of 2 lemons
1 kg sugar

First sterilise the jars. Place the hulled blackberries in a heavy based pan and mash slightly to extract some juice. Cook gently until soft. Add lemon juice and stir in the sugar until dissolved, then bring jam to a brisk boil. When setting point is reached, take from heat and pour into hot jars. Cover until cool, then seal.

BLACKCURRANT JAM

Makes 4 × 350 ml jars

---

1 kg blackcurrants
3 cups water
6 cups sugar

Sterilise the jars. Wash black-currants. Remove stalks. Put in a heavy based pan with the water. Bring to the boil. Simmer gently until fruit is soft. Stir in sugar until dissolved. Bring to boil and boil briskly until the setting point is reached. Pack in hot jars, cover until cool and seal.

BLUEBERRY JAM

Makes 3 × 350 ml jars

---

4 cups blueberries
3 cups water
5 cups sugar

Sterilise the jars. Top and tail blueberries. Put in a heavy based pan with water. Cook gently until berries are soft. Stir in sugar until it is dissolved. Rapidly boil until the mixture reaches setting point. Pour into hot jars, cover until warm, then seal.

> AVOID ADDING THE SUGAR TOO EARLY TO TOUGH-SKINNED FRUITS SUCH AS BLACKCURRANTS. THE SKIN WILL NOT SOFTEN AFTER THE SUGAR HAS BEEN ADDED

BOYSENBERRY JAM

Makes 4 × 350 ml jars

---

1 kg boysenberries (frozen will do)
2 large cooking apples
3 cups sugar

Sterilise the jars. If frozen, allow boysenberries to thaw at room temperature. Peel, core and slice apples. Put apples and sugar in a heavy based pan, heat to boiling point, stirring to dissolve the sugar. Add the boysenberries. Boil briskly until setting point is reached. Pour into hot jars. Cover until cool, then seal.

BOYSENBERRY AND PORT JAM

Makes 3 × 350 ml jars

---

1 kg boysenberries (frozen will do)
3 cups sugar
¼ cup port

Sterilise the jars. If frozen, allow the boysenberries to thaw in a pan at room temperature. Add sugar. Heat until boiling, and stir until the sugar dissolves. Bring to full boil, and continue to boil until setting point is reached. Remove from heat, and stir in port. Put in hot jars. Cover until cool, then seal.

CARROT AND DRIED APRICOT JAM

Makes 4 × 350 ml jars

250 g dried apricots
6 cups water
500 g carrots
7 cups sugar

In a non-metallic bowl soak apricots overnight in 2½ cups of the water. Next day, sterilise the jars, then boil washed, whole, unpeeled carrots in 3½ cups of water. Drain, reserving liquid. Grate the cooled carrots. Drain apricots and cook in the carrot water until pulpy. Mash. Add the grated carrot and sugar. Stir until sugar is dissolved. Boil until setting point is reached. Pack into hot jars, cover until cool and seal.

CHERRY JAM

Makes 7 × 350 ml jars

2 kg cherries
1.5 kg sugar
½ cup lemon juice

First sterilise the jars. Stone cherries. Tie stones in muslin bag. Put fruit and muslin bag in a heavy pan and simmer gently until the fruit is tender. Meanwhile warm the sugar in a low oven (130°C). Remove the muslin bag and add the warmed sugar and lemon juice. Stir until sugar dissolves. Rapidly boil until setting point is reached. Pour into hot jars, cover, cool, then seal.

CHOKO AND LEMON JAM

Makes 1 × 350 ml jar

2 chokos
1 lemon
½ teaspoon salt
¾ cup water
1¾ cups sugar
2 tablespoons finely chopped
   preserved ginger

Peel and quarter chokos. Remove seeds and grate flesh. Put grated choko in a non-metallic bowl with thinly sliced lemon and sprinkle salt over the top. Cover and stand overnight. Next day, sterilise the jar, then pour off any liquid in the choko bowl. Put water, sugar and ginger in pan and stir to dissolve. Bring to boil. Add chokos and lemon. Boil rapidly to setting point. Pour into hot jar, cover until cool, then seal.

CRABAPPLE AND GINGER JAM

Makes 6 × 350 ml jars

2 kg crabapples
1½ cups water
1 tablespoon finely chopped preserved
   ginger
sugar

Sterilise the jars. Wash and chop fruit. Put in pan with water. Cook until fruit is tender. Rub through a sieve and weigh pulp. Return pulp to the pan. Add the ginger. To each 600 g of pulp, add 500 g of sugar, stirring until it dissolves. Boil briskly until setting point is reached. Pack in hot jars, cover until cool and seal.

CRABAPPLE AND GUAVA JAM

Makes 4 × 350 ml jars

500 g crabapples
500 g guavas
water
sugar

Sterilise the jars. Wash both fruits and chop roughly. Place in a heavy based pan and just cover with water. Boil until the fruit is tender. Strain through sieve. Measure pulp and return it to the pan. Bring pulp to boil. Add 1 cup of sugar to each cup of pulp, stirring to dissolve. Boil briskly until setting point is reached. Put in hot jars. Cover until cool and seal.

DAMSON JAM

Makes 3 × 350 ml jars

1 kg damsons
4 cups sugar
1 orange

Wash damsons. Cut in half. Cover with sugar in a non-metallic bowl and let stand overnight. Next day, sterilise the jars, then slowly heat fruit mixture in a pan. Stir until sugar dissolves, then simmer until syrup thickens. Remove stones as they rise. Mince rind and flesh of orange, discarding pith, and add to pan. Boil hard to setting point. Pack in hot jars, cover until cool, then seal.

FEIJOA JAM

Makes 5 × 350 ml jars

1 kg feijoas, peeled and sliced
½ cup water
juice and rind of 1 lemon
1 kg sugar

First sterilise the jars. Put fruit and water in a heavy based pan with the lemon juice and rind. Boil until the fruit is soft. Add the sugar, stirring until the sugar has dissolved. Boil until setting point is reached. Pour into hot jars and cover until cool, then seal.

FIG JAM

Makes 5 × 350 ml jars

1 kg fresh, firm figs
juice and finely grated rind of 2
    lemons
4 cups sugar

Sterilise the jars. Top figs to remove the stem and quarter. Put figs in pan with lemon juice and rind. Cook gently until soft. If necessary, add 2 tablespoons of water. Stir in sugar until dissolved, then bring to rapid boil, until setting point is reached. Cool slightly. Stir and pour into hot jars. Cover until cool, then seal.

FIG AND GINGER JAM

Makes 3 × 350 ml jars

1.25 kg fresh, firm figs
1 kg sugar
½ cup vinegar
250 g crystallised ginger, sliced
¼ cup lemon juice
2 teaspoons grated lemon rind

Remove stems and quarter figs, and put in a large non-metallic bowl. Cover with sugar and let stand overnight. Next day, sterilise the jars, then put contents of bowl in a heavy based pan with vinegar, ginger, lemon juice and rind. Boil until setting point is reached. Pour into hot jars. Cover until cool, then seal.

FIG AND LEMON JAM

Makes 5 × 350 ml jars

---

1 kg green or purple figs
juice of 4 lemons
grated rind of 1 lemon
1 kg sugar

Sterilise the jars. Wash and quarter figs. Put in a heavy based pan with lemon juice and grated rind. Cook gently until the fruit is soft. Stir in the sugar until it dissolves, then bring to a rapid boil until setting point is reached. Cool slightly before pouring into hot jars. Cover until cool, then seal.

FIG AND ORANGE JAM

Makes 5 × 350 ml jars

---

1 kg green or purple figs
juice of 2 oranges
juice of 1 lemon
4 cups sugar

Sterilise the jars. Quarter figs. Put in a heavy based pan with orange and lemon juice and cook gently until fruit is soft. Stir in sugar until dissolved. Boil rapidly until the jam reaches setting point. Cool slightly before pouring into hot jars. Cover until cool then seal.

FRUIT SALAD JAM

Makes 4 × 350 ml jars

---

400 g apricots
400 g red plums
2 passionfruit
1 × 210 g can crushed pineapple
500 g ripe banana
2 tablespoons lemon juice
5¼ cups sugar

First sterilise the jars. Wash and halve apricots and plums. Discard stones. Put in a pan with passionfruit pulp, pineapple and syrup from can, sliced banana and lemon juice. Simmer until the fruit is soft. Add sugar and stir until dissolved. Boil briskly until setting point is reached. Let stand for 5 minutes. Pack into hot jars, cover until cool, then seal.

DRIED FRUIT JAM

Makes 6 × 350 ml jars

---

500 g mixed dried fruit
4¾ cups water
juice and grated rind of 1 orange
juice and grated rind of 1 lemon
1 kg sugar

In a non-metallic bowl soak the dried fruit in the water overnight. Next day, sterilise the jars, then put the fruit and liquid in a heavy pan, removing any stones. Add the orange and lemon juice and rind. Bring to boil. Simmer until the fruit is soft. Stir in the sugar until dissolved. Boil to setting point. Cool slightly before pouring into hot jars. Cover until cool, then seal.

GOOSEBERRY JAM

Makes 7 × 350 ml jars

1.5 kg gooseberries
2⅓ cups water
2 kg sugar

First sterilise the jars. Top and tail gooseberries. Wash and drain. Put in a heavy based pan with the water. Cook gently until the fruit is pulpy. Add the sugar and stir until it dissolves. Bring to a rapid boil until setting point is reached. Pour into hot jars. Cover until cool, then seal.

GOOSEBERRY AND ORANGE JAM

Makes 2 × 350 ml jars

---

500 g gooseberries
1 orange
25 g raisins
1¼ cups sugar

Sterilise the jars. Top and tail gooseberries. Put into a heavy based pan. Pare off orange rind and shred finely. Add to pan. Discard white pith from orange, chop orange flesh roughly and add to pan. Bring fruit to boil and simmer until tender. Add raisins. Stir in the sugar until completely dissolved. Boil briskly until the setting point is reached. Pack in hot jars, cover until cool, then seal.

CAPE GOOSEBERRY JAM

Makes 7 × 350 ml jars

1.5 kg cape gooseberries
1.5 kg sugar
1 cup water

Sterilise the jars. Halve cape gooseberries and place in pan with sugar and water. Bring to the boil. Continue boiling briskly for about 40 minutes. When setting point is reached pour into hot jars. Cover until cool, then seal.

BLACK GRAPE JAM

Makes 3 × 350 ml jars

1.5 kg black grapes
1½ cups water
sugar
juice of 1 lemon

Sterilise the jars. Wash grapes. Mash them a bit in pan. Add ½ cup of the water. Boil until seeds separate. Drain off the water and discard seeds. Separate the skins from the pulp and boil skins in remaining cup of water for 20 minutes. Measure the pulp with a cup measure before adding it to the skins, and continue boiling grape mixture until skins are tender. Then add ¼ cup of sugar to each cup of pulp. Add lemon juice. Boil briskly to setting point. Pack in hot jars, cover, cool and then seal.

GREEN GRAPE JAM

Makes 2 × 350 ml jars

---

1 kg green grapes
2 cups sugar
¼ cup lemon juice

Wash the grapes and remove stalks. Place in layers with sugar between each layer in a non-metallic bowl and let stand overnight. Next day, sterilise the jars, then put contents of bowl in a pan, add the lemon juice and bring to the boil. Stir frequently. Skim off the seeds when they rise to the surface. Then boil briskly to setting point. Pack in hot jars, cover until cool and seal.

GRAPE AND LEMON JAM

Makes 3 × 350 ml jars

1.5 kg grapes
1½ cups water
sugar
¼ cup lemon juice

Sterilise the jars. Wash grapes. Mash grapes a handful at a time, and remove skins. Put pulp in pan. Add ½ cup of the water and boil until seeds separate. Strain. Discard seeds. Boil skins for 20 minutes in remaining cup of water. Measure the amount of pulp with a cup measure before adding it to the skins and continue boiling mixture until the skins are tender. Add ¼ cup of sugar to each cup of pulp, and then add lemon juice. Stir to dissolve sugar, then boil briskly to setting point. Pack in hot jars, cover until cool and seal.

GREENGAGE JAM

Makes 8 × 350 ml jars

2.5 kg greengages
2½ cups water
2 kg sugar

Sterilise the jars. Halve and stone fruit. Extract 10 kernels from stones and blanch in some boiling water. After 5–10 minutes test a kernel. If the skin rubs off they are ready. Remove skins and slice. Put the fruit and the water in pan together with blanched kernels. Bring to the boil, reduce heat and simmer until fruit is soft. Stir in sugar until dissolved. Boil briskly until setting point is reached. Skim off foam before pouring into hot jars. Cover, and seal when cool.

GUAVA JAM

Makes 3 × 350 ml jars

---

500 g guavas
3–4 tablespoons water
sugar
juice of 1 lemon

First sterilise the jars. Wash the guavas and chop up roughly. Put in a heavy pan with water. Boil until the fruit is tender. Strain through a sieve, measure pulp and return it to the pan. Add 1 cup of sugar to each cup of pulp and stir in until it dissolves. Add lemon juice. Bring to brisk boil until setting point is reached. Pack in hot jars, cover until cool, then seal.

HARMONY JAM

Makes 5 × 350 ml jars

---

500 g peeled and cored eating apples
750 g peeled, cored and diced cooking pears
250 g stoned and quartered red plums
1 cup cold water
5 cups sugar

Sterilise the jars. Place apple peels and cores in a muslin bag. Cut flesh into small pieces. Put all

fruit, muslin bag and water in a heavy pan. Cook gently until fruit is soft. Do pectin test (see p. 10). If clot is firm, remove muslin bag. Squeeze out all liquid. If there is insufficient pectin, continue boiling and redo test in a few minutes, but be careful not to overcook. Stir in sugar until dissolved, then boil rapidly to setting point. Pour into hot jars, cover until cool, then seal.

HEDGEROW JAM

Makes 10 × 350 ml jars

---

1 kg crabapples or *cooking apples*
500 g blackberries
500 g elderberries
1.5 kg plums
2⅓ cups water
sugar

Sterilise the jars. Wash fruit. Chop apples. Put all fruit and water in pan. Cook until fruit is tender. Rub fruit and water it cooked in through a sieve and weigh pulp. Return the pulp to the pan. To each 600 g of pulp add 500 g of sugar, stirring until dissolved. Boil rapidly until setting point is reached. Pour into hot jars. Cover until cool, then seal.

AVOID USING OVER-RIPE FRUIT, DAMAGED OR BRUISED PIECES OF FRUIT, OR ANY DISEASED FRUIT

KIWIFRUIT JAM

Makes 3 × 350 ml jars

---

1 kg kiwifruit
3 tablespoons lemon juice
1 cup water
3 cups sugar

First sterilise the jars. Peel and roughly chop kiwifruit. Put in a heavy based pan with lemon juice and water. Boil until pulpy. Add sugar and stir until dissolved. Boil without stirring until setting point is reached. Pack in hot jars, cover until cool and seal.

FREEZER KIWIFRUIT JAM

Makes 5 × 100 ml jars

---

500 g frozen, whole kiwifruit
2¼ cups sugar
¼ teaspoon citric acid
⅔ cup pectin stock (see p. 10)

Sterilise the jars. Thaw kiwifruit and peel them. Purée fruit in blender, then put in bowl with sugar and citric acid. Stir well for 2 minutes. Let stand for 20 minutes. Stir once or twice until sugar dissolves. Add pectin. Stir for 3 minutes. Put in jars and let stand until set. Seal with wax. This jam keeps for 6 weeks in refrigerator, or 1 year in freezer. If you are going to freeze the jam, don't fill jars completely.

KIWIFRUIT AND GINGER JAM

Makes 3 × 350 ml jars

---

1 kg kiwifruit
3 tablespoons lemon juice
1 cup water
2 tablespoons finely chopped
  crystallised ginger
3 cups sugar

Sterilise the jars. Peel and chop kiwifruit roughly. Put in a heavy pan with lemon juice and water. Boil fruit to a pulp. Add ginger and stir in the sugar until it has dissolved. Boil briskly without stirring until setting point is reached. Pack in hot jars, cover until cool and seal.

LOQUAT JAM

Makes 3 × 350 ml jars

1.5 kg washed and seeded loquats
1 cup water
sugar
½ cup lemon juice

The loquats used for this jam must not be over-ripe. First sterilise the jars. Put seeded loquats in pan. Add water and cook until fruit is soft. Measure fruit mixture with cup measure and return to pan. Stir in ¾ cup of sugar to each cup of pulp and continue stirring until dissolved. Add lemon juice. Boil briskly until setting point is reached. Pack in hot jars, cover until cool and seal.

LYCHEE JAM

Makes 3 × 350 ml jars

2.5 kg lychees
water
sugar
½ cup lemon juice

First sterilise the jars. Cover lychees with boiling water and soak for 10 minutes. Rub off skins and remove stones. Weigh out 1.5 kg of fruit and put in pan with 1 cup of the soaking water. Cook until fruit is soft. Measure amount of pulp and stir in ¾ cup of sugar to each cup of pulp. When sugar is dissolved add lemon juice. Boil briskly until setting point is reached. Pack in hot jars, cover until cool and seal.

MELON JAM

Makes 6 × 350 ml jars

2.2 kg jam or pie melon
2 kg sugar
juice and rind of 2 lemons

Remove the seeds and the rind from the melon and dice into 2.5-cm pieces. Place in a non-metallic bowl with half of the sugar sprinkled over the top. Cover and leave to stand overnight. Next day, sterilise the jars, then transfer contents of bowl to a heavy based pan. Add the rest of the sugar and the lemon juice and rind. Boil until the mixture is clear and setting point is reached. Pack in hot jars, cover until cool and seal.

MARROW AND GINGER JAM

Makes 7 × 350 ml jars

1.5 kg marrow
1.5 kg sugar
25 g peeled root ginger
juice and rind of 2 lemons

Peel marrow. Remove seeds. Cut into cubes. In a large non-metallic bowl place marrow in layers with sugar. Let stand overnight. Next day, sterilise the jars, then tie ginger and lemon rind in muslin bag. Put in a pan with marrow and its juices. Sugar will be left at the bottom of the bowl, and reserve it to add later. Bring slowly to the boil, and then add lemon juice and sugar. Simmer until marrow is clear and syrup is thick. Pack in hot jars, cover until cool and seal.

MELON AND GINGER JAM

Makes 6 × 350 ml jars

2.2 kg jam or pie melon
juice and rind of 2 lemons
250 g preserved ginger, diced
2 kg sugar

Slice the melon and remove seeds and rind. Leave to stand overnight in a non-metallic bowl mixed with the lemon juice and rind, preserved ginger and sugar. Next day, sterilise the jars, then transfer contents of bowl to a heavy based pan and boil gently until setting point is reached. Pack into hot jars, cover until cool and seal.

MELON AND GOOSEBERRY JAM

Makes 4 × 350 ml jars

1.2 kg jam or pie melon
500 g gooseberries
¼ cup lemon juice
2 cups water
4 cups sugar

Peel the pie melon, remove seeds and mash or mince flesh. Crush gooseberries. Put fruit in a large non-metallic bowl. Add lemon juice and water. Stir. Leave to stand, covered, overnight. Next day, sterilise the jars first, then transfer contents of bowl to pan. Add sugar, stir to dissolve and boil gently until setting point is reached, stirring to prevent sticking. Pack in hot jars, cover until cool and seal.

MELON AND LEMON JAM

Makes 6 × 350 ml jars

2.2 kg jam or pie melon
2.2 kg sugar
5 cups water
4 lemons, thinly sliced
½ teaspoon citric acid

First sterilise the jars. Peel, deseed and dice melon. Make syrup by boiling sugar and water together for 10 minutes, stirring, until a pale honey colour. Add melon, lemon and citric acid. Boil for 1½–2 hours, testing for setting after 1½ hours. Pour into hot jars. Cover until cool, and then seal.

MELON AND PASSIONFRUIT JAM

Makes 6 × 350 ml jars

2.2 kg jam or pie melon
8 cups sugar
24 passionfruit
½ cup lemon juice

Remove rind and seed from melon and grate flesh finely. Place in a non-metallic bowl with half the sugar. Let stand, covered, overnight. Next day, sterilise the jars, then transfer contents of bowl to a heavy pan and bring to slow boil until clear. Add passionfruit pulp, rest of sugar and lemon juice. Boil briskly to setting point. Pack in hot jars, cover until cool and seal.

MELON AND PINEAPPLE JAM

Makes 10 × 350 ml jars

3.2 kg jam or pie melon
4 lemons
2 kg sugar
2 × 850 g cans preserved pineapple
   or 1 kg diced fresh pineapple flesh

Peel, deseed and cut up melon and place in a non-metallic bowl. Add finely sliced lemons, cover with sugar and let stand, covered, overnight. (If fresh pineapple is to be used, allow 3 kg of sugar instead of 2 kg.) Next day, sterilise the jars. Transfer contents of bowl to a heavy based pan. Finely cut up pineapple and add to pan. Boil for 2½ hours, or until setting point is reached. Pour into hot jars. Cover until cool and seal.

MULBERRY JAM

Makes 3 × 350 ml jars

2 large cooking apples, peeled and cored
450 g mulberries, stalks removed
½ cup water
500 g sugar

First sterilise the jars. Chop apples. In a heavy based pan bring mulberries, apple and water to the boil over low heat. Cover pan and cook until fruit is pulpy. Stir in sugar until dissolved. Bring to a brisk boil. Do not stir. Boil to setting point. Skim foam off the surface before pouring into hot jars. Cover until cool and then seal.

NECTARINE JAM

Makes 3 × 350 ml jars

1.5 kg nectarines
2 teaspoons grated orange rind
¼ cup orange juice
¼ cup lemon juice
5 cups sugar
½ cup slivered almonds
6 tablespoons pectin stock (see p. 10)

Sterilise the jars. Wash and stone fruit. Dice into 1-cm cubes and put in pan. Add grated rind, juices and

sugar and mix well. Bring to boil quickly, stirring all the time, and then boil for 7 minutes without stirring. Stir in slivered almonds and pectin and boil to setting point. Pack, cover, and seal when cool.

SPECIAL NECTARINE JAM

Makes 5 × 350 ml jars

1.25 kg nectarines
½ cup orange juice
1 tablespoon lemon juice
1½ teaspoons grated orange rind
½ cup slivered almonds
5 cups sugar
½ cup pectin stock (see p. 10)

Sterilise the jars. Wash, dry and stone fruit. Cut into small pieces. Put in a heavy based pan. Add juices, grated rind and slivered almonds. Bring to boil. Stir in sugar until dissolved. Boil hard for 1 minute. Remove from heat and stand for 20 minutes. Pack in hot jars, cover until cool and seal. This jam is best kept refrigerated. It has a short life otherwise.

A QUICK WAY TO TOP AND TAIL GOOSEBERRIES IS TO USE A SHARP PAIR OF SCISSORS

STORE YOUR PRESERVES IN A COOL, AIRY, DRY, DARK PLACE

NECTARINE AND ORANGE JAM

Makes 3 × 350 ml jars

1 × 1 litre jar nectarines in syrup
1 orange
sugar

Sterilise the jars. Drain nectarines and weigh them. Reserve the syrup. Peel orange and chop rind finely. Squeeze orange for juice. Place orange rind, juice and pulp in pan with 1 cup of reserved fruit syrup. Simmer gently for 20 minutes. Add nectarines. Boil until fruit has pulped. To each 500 g of nectarines originally weighed, add 1¾ cups of sugar. Stir until dissolved and then boil briskly until it jells – you will be able to see this in the pan and won't need to do a setting test. Pour into hot jars, cover, and seal when cool.

PEACH JAM

Makes 2 × 350 ml jars

1 kg peaches
1 cup water
2 tablespoons lemon juice
¾ kg sugar

First sterilise the jars. Peel and stone peaches. Put in pan with water. Cover. Cook gently until fruit is soft. Add lemon juice. Stir in sugar until dissolved. Increase the heat and boil briskly until setting point is reached. Cool slightly before pouring into hot jars. Cover and leave to cool, then seal.

PEACH AND BRANDY JAM

Makes 6 × 250 ml jars

750 g fully ripe peaches
550 g sugar
1 tablespoon lemon juice
1 teaspoon grated lemon rind
½ cup slivered almonds
1 cinnamon stick
¼ cup glacé cherries
½ cup pectin stock (see p. 10)
3 tablespoons brandy

Sterilise the jars. Peel, stone and chop peaches, collecting all the juice. Put flesh and juice in pan with sugar, lemon juice and rind, almonds, cinnamon and cherries. Bring to boil, then remove cinnamon stick. Stir until sugar dissolves. Remove from heat and stir in pectin stock and brandy. Let stand for 5 minutes. Stir again before pouring into hot jars. Cover until cool, then seal.

PEACH AND PEAR JAM

Makes 6 × 250 ml jars

500 g peaches
500 g cooking pears
water
juice and grated rind of 2 lemons
1 kg sugar

First sterilise the jars. Skin and stone peaches. Peel and core pears. Chop both into even-sized bits. Put in a heavy based pan with just enough water to cover the bottom of the pan. Simmer gently. Add lemon juice and rind. Stir in sugar until dissolved. Boil briskly to setting point. Pour into hot jars. Cover until cool, then seal.

PEACH AND PINEAPPLE JAM

Makes 7 × 350 ml jars

3.5 kg yellow peaches
1 pineapple
3 kg sugar
juice of 2 lemons

Sterilise the jars. Peel and stone peaches. Pare and chop pineapple. Put fruit in a heavy based pan with just enough water to stop catching. Heat slowly to a simmer, and cook gently for 30 minutes. Stir in sugar until dissolved. Add juice of lemons. Boil gently to setting point. Pack in hot jars, cover until cool and seal.

PEACH AND PLUM JAM

Makes 4 × 350 ml jars

500 g peeled, halved and stoned
    peaches
2.5 kg halved and stoned plums
1 cup water
3 cups sugar

First sterilise the jars. Put fruit in a heavy based pan with water. Cook gently until soft. Add sugar, stirring until dissolved. Bring to hard boil and continue boiling to setting point. Pack in hot jars, cover until cool and seal.

DRIED PEACH JAM

Makes 10 × 350 ml jars

500 g dried peaches
boiling water
1 teaspoon bicarbonate of soda
8 cups water
juice of 2 lemons
2.25 kg sugar

Place peaches in a non-metallic bowl. Cover them with boiling water in which 1 teaspoon of bicarbonate of soda has been dissolved. Soak for 30 minutes, rub peaches to clean, rinse and place them in the 8 cups of water. Soak for 24 hours. Next day, sterilise the jars. Place peaches and water in pan. Add lemon juice. Boil gently until fruit softens. Add sugar. Boil to a good consistency. Cool slightly before packing into jars. Cover until cool, then seal.

PEAR JAM

Makes 8 × 350 ml jars

1.5 kg sugar
4 cups water
2 kg cooking pears
juice and grated rind of 3 lemons

Sterilise the jars. Place sugar and water in pan. Stir to dissolve over gentle heat, then boil to a syrup (about 10 minutes). Peel, core and cut up pears. Add pears, lemon juice and rind to the syrup. Simmer until fruit is clear and setting point is reached. Pack in hot jars, cover until cool and seal.

PEAR JAM WITH BRANDY

Makes 8 × 350 ml jars

1.5 kg sugar
4 cups water
2 kg cooking pears
juice and grated rind of 3 lemons
2 tablespoons Napoleon brandy

Sterilise the jars. Place the sugar and water in a pan, stir to dissolve over gentle heat, then boil to a syrup (about 10 minutes). Peel, core and cut up the pears. Add to syrup with lemon juice and rind. Simmer until fruit is clear and setting point is reached. Remove from heat and stir in the brandy. Pack in hot jars, cover until cool, then seal.

PEAR AND GINGER JAM

Makes 11 × 350 ml jars

3.5 kg cooking pears
2.5-cm piece peeled and crushed root ginger
juice and thinly pared rind of 3 lemons
4 cups water
2.5 kg sugar

First sterilise the jars. Peel, core and quarter pears. Put peels, cores, ginger and lemon rind in a muslin bag. Put bag, pears and water in a heavy pan. Bring to boil and simmer until the fruit is soft. Remove the bag, squeezing out any liquid. Stir in sugar until dissolved. Add lemon juice and boil to the setting point. Stand for 5 minutes before packing in jars. Cover until cool and seal.

PERSIMMON JAM

Makes 4 × 350 ml jars

2.5 kg persimmons
¼ cup lemon juice
1 kg sugar
1 cup water (if necessary)

Sterilise the jars. Cut persimmons in half and remove seeds. Scoop out pulp and discard skins. Whirl the pulp in a blender until smooth, or press through a sieve. Place in a heavy based pan the fruit purée, lemon juice, sugar and water if necessary – if the persimmons are juicy you may not need to use all or any water. Stir to dissolve sugar, then boil rapidly to setting point. Pack in hot jars, cover until cool and then seal.

PINEAPPLE JAM

Amount depends on fruit size

---

1 pineapple
sugar
1–2 lemons

Peel pineapple. Weigh the flesh and grate coarsely. Put in a non-metallic bowl with an equal weight of sugar and the juice and rind of 1 lemon. If the pineapple is large, the juice of a second lemon can be used. Cover and let stand overnight. Next day, sterilise the jars, then transfer contents of bowl to a heavy based pan. Boil briskly to setting point. Pack in hot jars, cover until cool and then seal.

PLUM JAM

Makes 3 × 350 ml jars

1 kg red plums
1 kg sugar

Wash and dry plums. Chop roughly and remove stones. Leave overnight in a non-metallic bowl, covered with the sugar. Next day, sterilise the jars and transfer contents of bowl to a heavy pan. Bring to boil, stirring until the sugar dissolves. Boil rapidly until setting point is reached. Pack in hot jars, cover until cool and then seal.

PLUM AND ORANGE JAM

Makes 8 × 350 ml jars

750 g plums
750 g cooking apples
1¼ cups water
juice and rind of 2 oranges
5 cups sugar

First sterilise the jars. Halve and stone plums. Peel, core and slice apples. Put in a heavy pan with water, orange juice and rind. Bring to boil, then reduce heat and simmer until fruit is soft. Stir in the sugar until it dissolves, then boil until setting point is reached. Remove from heat and skim off any foam before packing in hot jars. Cover until cool and seal.

PLUM AND PASSIONFRUIT JAM

Makes 2 × 350 ml jars

6 passionfruit
500 g stoned plums
water
sugar

Sterilise the jars. Put passionfruit pulp aside and cover skins with water in pan. Simmer until skins are soft. Remove from heat, reserving water. Scoop out pith from skins and add to pulp. Put pith and pulp in pan with stoned plums. Add 1 cup of the reserved water. Simmer until fruit is soft. Remove from heat and measure amount of fruit pulp with cup measure. Return to the pan and add ¾ cup of sugar to each cup of pulp. Stir until sugar has dissolved over gentle heat, then boil until set. Pack and seal when cool.

DON'T FORGET TO LABEL AND DATE YOUR PRESERVES

A GOOD-SIZED ORANGE WILL GIVE ABOUT 5 TABLESPOONS OF JUICE, WHILE AN AVERAGE-SIZED LEMON WILL GIVE ABOUT 3 TABLESPOONS OF JUICE

PLUM JAM WITH PORT

Makes 3 × 350 ml jars

---

1 kg blood plums
1 cup water
3 cups sugar
¼ cup port

First sterilise the jars. Wash plums, halve and remove stones. Put in a heavy based pan with water. Boil until the fruit is pulpy. Turn down heat and stir in the sugar until dissolved. Return to a brisk boil until setting point is reached. Remove from heat and stir in the port. Pour into hot jars. Cover until cool and then seal.

PLUM AND RAISIN JAM

Makes 3 × 350 ml jars

---

500 g plum pulp (frozen will do)
½ cup raisins
1½ cups sugar
¼ cup slivered almonds

First sterilise the jars. If using frozen plums, let pulp thaw at room temperature. Finely chop raisins. Place pulp and raisins in a heavy pan. Heat until boiling. Stir in the sugar until dissolved. Cook until thick and the setting point is reached. Stir in the almonds. Let stand a few minutes before packing in hot jars. Cover until cool, then seal.

PLUM AND RUM JAM

Makes 5 × 350 ml jars

---

2 kg red plums
2 cups water
5 cups sugar
3 tablespoons Jamaican dark rum

First sterilise the jars. Stone plums. Put in a heavy based pan with water and simmer until the fruit is very soft. Stir in the sugar over low heat until it dissolves, then boil briskly until the setting point is reached. Stir occasionally as the mixture thickens. Remove from heat and add the rum. Pour into hot jars. Cover until cool and then seal.

PLUM AND SHERRY JAM

Makes 5 × 350 ml jars

---

2 kg plums
2 cups water
5 cups sugar
1 cup sweet sherry

Sterilise the jars. Stone plums. Put in a heavy based pan with water. Simmer until the fruit is very soft, then stir in the sugar over low heat to dissolve. Turn up heat and boil rapidly until the setting point is reached, stirring often as the jam thickens. Remove from heat and add the sherry. Pack into hot jars, cover until cool and seal.

PLUM JAM WITH WHISKY

Makes 5 × 350 ml jars

2 kg red plums
2 cups water
5 cups sugar
juice of 2 lemons
grated rind of 1 lemon
1/2 cup whisky

Sterilise the jars. Stone plums. Put in a heavy based pan with water. Simmer until the fruit is very soft. Over low heat stir in the sugar until dissolved, then add lemon juice and rind. Boil briskly until the setting point is reached, stirring often as the jam thickens. Remove from heat and add the whisky. Pack into hot jars. Cover until cool, then seal.

QUINCE JAM

Makes 5 × 350 ml jars

2 kg quinces
water
sugar
juice of 2 lemons

First sterilise the jars. Peel, core and chop quinces into small cubes. Put into a heavy pan, cover with water and simmer until soft. Measure pulp with cup measure. To each cup allow 250 g of sugar. Return pulp to pan with sugar and lemon juice. Stir over low heat until the sugar dissolves, then boil rapidly until setting point is reached. Pour into hot jars and cover until cool, then seal.

RASPBERRY JAM

Makes 7 × 350 ml jars

1.5 kg raspberries
1.5 kg sugar

First sterilise the jars. Put raspberries in a heavy based pan. Heat gently, stirring occasionally until boiling. Stir in the sugar over low heat until dissolved, then boil briskly until the setting point is reached. Pour into hot jars and cover until cool, then seal.

RED-CURRANT JAM

Makes 7 × 350 ml jars

1 kg red currants
3 cups water
6 cups sugar

Sterilise the jars. Remove stalks from red currants. Put fruit and water in a heavy based pan. Bring to the boil and simmer gently until fruit is soft and pulpy. Stir in the sugar until it dissolves, then boil rapidly until setting point is reached, stirring occasionally. Cool slightly before packing. Cover, and seal when cool.

RHUBARB JAM

Makes 6 × 350 ml jars

1.5 kg rhubarb
6 cups sugar
juice and grated rind of 2 lemons
3 cooking apples

Cut rhubarb into 2.5-cm lengths. In a non-metallic bowl put alternate layers of sugar and rhubarb. Add lemon juice and rind. Let stand overnight, covered. Next day, sterilise the jars. Transfer the contents of the bowl to a heavy based pan. Peel, core and chop apples. Place in pan. Bring slowly to the boil, stirring until sugar dissolves. Then boil rapidly to setting point, stirring occasionally. Remove scum before pouring into hot jars. Cover, and seal when cool.

RHUBARB AND APPLE JAM

Makes 12 × 350 ml jars

1.5 kg rhubarb
1 kg cooking apples
juice of 1 lemon
1 cup water
6 cups sugar
1 tablespoon chopped preserved ginger

Sterilise the jars. Cut rhubarb into 2.5-cm pieces. Peel, core and slice apples. Place rhubarb, apple, lemon juice and water in a heavy pan. Bring to boil, then reduce heat and simmer. Stir often until fruit is soft. Stir in sugar until dissolved. Add ginger and boil briskly until setting point is reached. Pour into hot jars and cover until cool, then seal.

RHUBARB AND GINGER JAM

Makes 8 × 350 ml jars

2 kg rhubarb
1 cup water
juice of 1 lemon
5-cm piece peeled and crushed root ginger
6 cups sugar
5 tablespoons chopped preserved ginger

First sterilise the jars. Chop rhubarb into 2.5-cm pieces. Put rhubarb, water and lemon juice in a pan. Bring to boil. Add root ginger. Reduce heat and simmer. Stir often until rhubarb is soft. Remove root ginger. Stir in sugar until dissolved. Add preserved ginger. Boil briskly until setting point is reached. Pour into hot jars and cover. Seal when cool.

WHEN USING THE RIND OF A LEMON, ORANGE OR GRAPEFRUIT, TAKE CARE NOT TO USE THE PITH BECAUSE IT WILL GIVE A BITTER TASTE

DON'T FORGET TO LABEL AND DATE YOUR PRESERVES

RHUBARB AND ORANGE JAM

Makes 4 × 350 ml jars

---

1 kg rhubarb
½ cup water
grated rind of 1 orange
¼ cup orange juice
½ cup chopped preserved ginger
6 cups sugar
½ cup pectin stock (see p. 10)

Sterilise the jars. Cut rhubarb into thin slices. Put in a heavy based pan with the water, orange rind and juice. Cover and simmer until rhubarb is soft. Add ginger. Stir in the sugar until dissolved. Bring to boil for 3 minutes. Remove from heat and stir in pectin. Pour into hot jars, cover, cool, then seal.

RHUBARB AND STRAWBERRY JAM

Makes 6 × 350 ml jars

---

500 g rhubarb
500 g strawberries
4½ cups sugar

Wash and trim rhubarb. Cut in small pieces. Hull, wash and halve strawberries. Put fruit in a non-metallic bowl and cover with 3 cups of sugar. Let stand overnight. Next day, sterilise the jars, then transfer contents of bowl to a large pan. Add remaining sugar. Bring slowly to boil, stirring to dissolve sugar, then briskly boil, stirring occasionally, to setting point. Put in hot jars, cover, cool, then seal.

RHUBARB AND PINEAPPLE JAM

Makes 2 × 350 ml jars

---

500 g rhubarb
1 × 225 g can crushed pineapple
2½ cups sugar
1 × 106 g packet raspberry jelly
*   crystals*

Sterilise the jars. Wash and cut rhubarb into small bits. Put in a pan with pineapple and sugar and boil for 10 minutes. Remove from heat and stir in jelly crystals. Return to heat, and boil for a further 15 minutes. Pack in hot jars, cover and let cool, then seal.

ROCKMELON AND ORANGE JAM

Makes 3 × 175 ml jars

---

600 g peeled and seeded rockmelon or
*   cantaloup melon*
2½ cups sugar
½ cup orange juice
2 tablespoons grated orange rind

Finely dice melon. Put in a non-metallic bowl and cover with half the sugar. Let stand overnight, covered. Next day, sterilise the jars, then put contents of bowl in a heavy based pan with remaining sugar, orange juice and rind. Stir over low heat until sugar dissolves and then boil until setting point, mashing the melon to distribute evenly. Pack in hot jars, cover and let cool, then seal.

STRAWBERRY JAM

Makes 3 × 350 ml jars

1 kg strawberries
6 cups sugar
1½ teaspoons tartaric acid

First sterilise the jars. Wash and hull strawberries. Put in pan and crush lightly. Stir in sugar and bring to full rolling boil. Boil for 5 minutes. Stir in tartaric acid, and boil for 6 minutes from when jam returns to the boil. Pack in hot jars, cover and stand until cool, then seal.

STRAWBERRY AND GOOSEBERRY JAM

Makes 2 × 350 ml jars

250 g strawberries
250 g gooseberries
¼ cup water
1 tablespoon lemon juice
1½ cups sugar

Sterilise the jars. Wash and hull strawberries. Wash, top and tail gooseberries. Place the gooseberries and water in a pan and boil gently until soft. Add strawberries and cook until soft. Stir in lemon juice and sugar until dissolved. Keep at rolling boil until jam reaches setting point. Pack in hot jars, cover until cool and seal.

STRAWBERRY AND GREEN APPLE JAM

Makes 2 × 350 ml jars

250 g peeled, cored and roughly
    chopped green apples
¼ cup water
250 g strawberries
1 tablespoon lemon juice
1½ cups sugar

Sterilise the jars. Put apples in a heavy pan with water. Simmer until soft. Wash and hull strawberries. Add to the apples and cook until pulpy. Stir in lemon juice and sugar until dissolved. Keep at rolling boil until jam reaches setting point. Pack in hot jars, cover and let cool, then seal.

STRAWBERRY AND PINEAPPLE JAM

Makes 3 × 350 ml jars

1 kg strawberries frozen in sugar
1 × 420 g can crushed pineapple
2½ cups sugar

Sterilise the jars. Thaw strawberries for an hour or so at room temperature. Place in a pan with the crushed pineapple. Allow to simmer, uncovered, for 3–5 minutes. Lower heat and stir in the sugar until it is dissolved. Then boil briskly until the setting point is reached. Pack into hot jars. Cover and let cool, then seal.

STRAWBERRY AND ROSE JAM

Makes 1 × 250 ml jar

¾ cup hulled strawberries
1¼ cups fragrant rose petals, firmly
* packed*
1 cup sugar
pinch of cream of tartar
½ cup water
1 tablespoon lemon juice

Sterilise the jar. Wash and halve strawberries. Cut off white ends of rose petals, wash and dry petals, and put in a heavy pan with sugar, cream of tartar, water and lemon juice. Add strawberries. Stir well over low heat until sugar dissolves, then boil briskly to setting point. Pack in hot jar, cover to cool, then seal.

TAMARILLO JAM

Makes 6 × 350 ml jars

---

500 g cooking apples
1.5 kg tamarillos
2 cups water
2 kg sugar
juice of 1 lemon

Sterilise the jars. Peel, core and mince apples. Scald tamarillos, peel and cut up. Place apples and tamarillos in pan with water. Bring to boil. Reduce heat and stir in the sugar until it is dissolved. Bring back to brisk boil until the setting point is reached. Add lemon juice. Pack in hot jars, cover and let cool, then seal.

TOMATO AND LEMON JAM

Makes 6 × 250 ml jars

1.5 kg tomatoes
500 g cooking apples
1 tablespoon grated lemon rind
⅓ cup lemon juice
1.25 kg sugar

First sterilise the jars. Skin tomatoes by covering with boiling water for 30 seconds. The skins will then remove easily. Cut tomatoes into thin slices and put in a heavy based pan. Peel, core and thinly slice apples. Add to pan with the lemon rind and bring to boil. Stir in lemon juice and sugar until dissolved. Boil briskly to setting point, stirring occasionally. Pour into hot jars. Cover and let cool, then seal.

A QUICK WAY TO TOP AND TAIL GOOSEBERRIES IS TO USE A SHARP PAIR OF SCISSORS

STORE YOUR PRESERVES IN A COOL, AIRY, DRY, DARK PLACE

CONSERVES

Conserves are jams in which the fruit is whole or in pieces. In the making of conserves, the fruit does not cook to pulp. It either remains whole or in the pieces it has been cut into, so small fruits are very suitable. The fruit stays suspended in a syrup that is not set as stiffly as jam. Conserves are richer than jams, but have a shorter shelf-life, and are best used within 6 months of making. They are delicious on scones or bread, they can be used as sauces on ice-creams and puddings, and they make delectable fillings for sponges. They may be flavoured with brandy, rum or other alcohol, added just towards the end of the cooking time. Kirsch complements the flavour of cherry or pineapple conserve, but it should be added with the sugar. Towards the end of the cooking time you can also add some diced, crystallised or preserved ginger to apples, pears or marrow, or a few raisins may be added to plums. There are two methods of preparing conserves (see following page).

METHOD 1

---

*2 cups fruit (preferably whole small
    apricots, small plums, halved
    peaches, fresh green figs, or
    cranberries)*
⅔ cup water
2 cups sugar
juice of 1 lemon

This method involves using a syrup
made of sugar and water. Prepare
the fruit. Over low heat gently
simmer the water, sugar and lemon
juice in a pan until the sugar has
dissolved. Add the fruit and cook
steadily until the fruit is just tender
and the syrup is thick.

METHOD 2

---

*fruit or vegetables (preferably diced
    cooking apples, diced cooking
    pears, diced pineapple, halved
    apricots, halved Victoria plums,
    halved feijoas, sliced mango, sliced
    guavas, black cherries, small
    strawberries, peeled and diced
    pumpkin or marrow)*
sugar
lemon juice

This method involves no water.
Use the amounts of fruit and sugar
given in the appropriate jam recipes.
Sprinkle the sugar over the fruit,
and allow to stand for several hours.
Then put all into a pan and stir
over a gentle heat until the sugar
has dissolved. Add lemon juice if it
is included in the jam recipe. Bring
to the boil, and continue boiling
fairly rapidly (watch that it does
not boil over) until the mixture is
lightly set. Stir occasionally, but
not too often, as stirring will lower
the temperature. The quicker it
reaches setting point, the better
will be the colour and flavour.
Overcooking will spoil both.

JELLIES

Jelly makes a delicious change from jam, but the process is longer and the yield is smaller. Fruit for making jelly should be mature and ripe, but not over-ripe. A good jelly should be clear, of good colour, and have a firm, even texture that is inclined to shake, but should retain most of its shape when broken. Jelly should have a rich, distinctive flavour.

Wash and drain all fruit. Cut away any bruised or damaged parts. Leave in all rinds, cores, stalks or stones, as these are a valuable source of pectin and improve the setting quality of the jellies. Fruit that is large or contains stones should be roughly chopped.

Cherries, gooseberries, melons, quinces and strawberries will make jelly or jam provided that some acid – usually lemon juice – is added. Fruits that jelly well with the addition of a little pectin (usually apple) are apricots, ripe blackberries, kiwifruit and guavas. For guava jelly, very little water should be used. If fruit needs added acid or pectin, often just an apple, or cores and peelings, boiled with the fruit, and lemon juice added to the strained juice, are enough.

Berries and small soft fruits need about 4 cups of water added to every 1.5 kg of fruit. Firm fruits like apples, japonicas or guavas need about 7 cups of water to each 1.5 kg of fruit. Very firm fruit like lemons, oranges or quinces needs about 15 cups of water to each 1.5 kg of fruit. After boiling to a pulp, the mixture is strained through a jelly bag, ideally overnight.

The resulting measured juice is the guide for the amount of sugar to add. For most of the good jelly-making fruits, add 1 cup of sugar to every cup of juice. For fruits with poorer jellying properties, to every cup of juice add ¾ cup of sugar. The mixture is then boiled as for jam until setting point is reached, and is packed in the same way.

APPLE JELLY

Makes 4 × 350 ml jars

1.75 kg cooking apples
7 cups cold water
sugar

Cut up apples, discarding any bruised bits. Put in a heavy based pan with water. Bring to the boil and simmer until very soft. Mash. Strain through jelly bag, leaving overnight if possible. Next day sterilise the jars, then measure juice and return it to pan. Stir in 1 cup of sugar to each cup of juice. Heat gently until it dissolves. Boil rapidly to setting point. Remove scum. Pour into hot jars, cover and let cool, then seal.

APPLE AND GINGER JELLY

Makes 4 × 250 ml jars

1.5 kg cooking apples
2-cm piece peeled root ginger
water
sugar

Wash apples. Cut into chunks. Slice ginger. Put apples and ginger in pan and just cover with water. Bring to boil, cook until pulpy and then strain through a jelly bag overnight. Next day sterilise the jars. Measure juice and return to pan. Stir in 1 cup of sugar to each cup of juice and continue stirring until dissolved. Boil briskly to setting point. Pack in hot jars, cover and let cool, then seal.

BLACKBERRY JELLY

Makes 6 × 250 ml jars

---

500 g cooking apples
1.25 kg blackberries
2½ cups water
4 cups sugar

Wash apples. Cut into chunks. Put in a heavy pan with blackberries and water. Bring to boil. Simmer until very soft. Mash, then strain through jelly bag overnight. Next day sterilise the jars and put juice in pan. Heat gently. Stir in sugar until dissolved. Boil rapidly until setting point is reached. Pour into hot jars. Cover while hot, and seal when cool.

CRABAPPLE JELLY

Makes 2 × 250 ml jars

---

5 cups crabapples
3 cups water
sugar

Wash fruit. Chop roughly, including skins and seeds. Put in pan. Add the water. Boil uncovered until the fruit is very soft. Strain through jelly bag overnight. Do not squeeze. Next day sterilise the jars. Measure juice and return to pan. Add ¾ cup of sugar to every cup of juice, stirring to dissolve. Boil briskly until setting point is reached. Pack in hot jars, cover and let cool, then seal.

ELDERBERRY JELLY

Makes 10 × 350 ml jars

---

1 kg elderberries
3 kg cooking apples
water
sugar

Take the elderberries off stems and put in a pan. Wash apples and cut into pieces. Put into pan with elderberries. Just cover with cold water. Bring to boil, then simmer until the fruit is pulpy. Strain through a jelly bag overnight. Next day sterilise the jars. Measure juice and return to pan. Add 1 cup of sugar to each cup of juice. When sugar dissolves, boil to setting point. Pack in hot jars, cover and let cool, then seal.

GOOSEBERRY JELLY

Makes 10 × 350 ml jars

---

2 kg gooseberries
7½ cups water
sugar

Wash gooseberries. Put in a pan with water. Bring to the boil. Reduce heat and simmer until fruit is very soft. Mash well. Strain through jelly bag overnight. Next day sterilise the jars. Measure juice and return to pan. Add 2 cups of sugar to each 2½ cups of juice. When sugar is dissolved, boil briskly until setting point is reached. Pack, cover, and seal when cool.

GOOSEBERRY AND CRABAPPLE JELLY

Makes 2 × 250 ml jars

---

600 g gooseberries
400 g crabapples
water
sugar

Wash fruit. Place in a pan. Cover with water and bring to boil. Simmer until the fruit is pulpy. Strain through jelly bag overnight. Next day sterilise the jars. Measure juice and return to pan. Add 1 cup of sugar to each cup of juice. Stir to dissolve sugar, then bring to the boil. Boil briskly to setting point. Pack and cover. Seal when cool.

GOOSEBERRY AND RASPBERRY JELLY

Makes 5 × 350 ml jars

---

900 g gooseberries
2¼ cups water
1.5 kg raspberries
sugar

Wash gooseberries. Put in pan and add the water. Simmer until the fruit is soft. Wash raspberries, put in another pan and simmer for 20 minutes. Mix the fruits, then strain through jelly bag overnight. Next day sterilise the jars. Measure juice and return to pan. Add 450 g of sugar to every 2¼ cups of juice. Stir to dissolve sugar, then boil briskly to setting point. Pack into jars. Cover, and seal when cool.

GRAPE JELLY

Makes 4 × 250 ml jars

---

6 cups black grapes
2 cooking apples
4 cups water
sugar
¼ cup lemon juice

Wash grapes. Roughly cut up apples without peeling or coring. Put fruit and water in a heavy based pan. Boil until mixture is very soft. Strain through jelly bag overnight. Next day sterilise the jars. Measure liquid and return to pan. Add ¾ cup of sugar to each cup of liquid, stirring to dissolve. Add lemon juice. Boil briskly to setting point. Pack in hot jars, cover, and seal when cool.

GRAPE AND LEMON JELLY

Makes 6 × 250 ml jars

---

2 kg grapes
3 lemons
6 cups water
sugar

Wash grapes. Put in pan with thinly sliced lemons and water. Cook until the grape skins separate. Strain through a jelly bag overnight. Next day sterilise the jars. Measure juice and pour into a heavy based pan. Add ¾ cup of sugar to each cup of liquid, stirring to dissolve. Boil briskly to setting point. Remove from heat. Stand a few minutes. Pack in hot jars, cover, and seal when cool.

GUAVA JELLY

Makes 8 × 350 ml jars

---

2 kg guavas, washed and quartered
¾ cup water
sugar
lime juice

Put guavas in a heavy based pan with water. Bring to boil over high heat. Reduce heat. Simmer until tender. Strain through a jelly bag overnight. Next day sterilise the jars. Measure juice and return to pan. Add 2 cups of sugar and 1 teaspoon of lime juice to each 2½ cups of juice. Over low heat stir in sugar. When dissolved, boil to setting point. Pack in hot jars, cover, and seal when cool.

HERB JELLY

Makes 4 × 250 ml jars

1.5 kg cooking apples
2⅓ cups white wine vinegar
5 cups water
sugar
chopped herb (¼ cup to each cup apple juice)
a few drops food colouring (optional)

Sage, thyme, parsley, mint and rosemary jellies can be made with this recipe. Serve sage jelly with pork, thyme jelly with poultry, parsley jelly with ham, and mint or rosemary jelly with lamb.

Wash and chop apples, including skins and cores. Put in pan with the vinegar and water. Bring to the boil and simmer until the apples are very soft. Strain overnight through a jelly bag. Next day sterilise the jars. Measure juice and return to the pan. Add 200 g of sugar to each cup of juice. Heat gently, stirring until the sugar has dissolved. Boil rapidly until the jelly point is reached. Then stir in the chopped herb and the food colouring. Remove any scum. Let cool slightly, then stir again before pouring into hot jars. Cover until cool, then seal.

LOQUAT JELLY

Makes 2 × 250 ml jars

1.5 kg loquats
pinch of salt
water
sugar
lemon juice

Fruit must not be too ripe or the result will be runny. Cut up fruit. Remove and discard seeds from three-quarters of the fruit. Put all fruit in pan, add salt and cover with water. Boil gently for 2 hours. Transfer to non-metallic bowl, cover and stand overnight. Next day sterilise the jars. Then return loquats to pan and boil gently for 1 hour. Strain through jelly bag. Measure juice and return to the pan. Add 2 cups of sugar and ¼ cup of lemon juice to each 2 cups of loquat juice. Stir to dissolve sugar, then boil until setting point is reached. Pack in hot jars, cover until cool, then seal.

JAPONICA JELLY

Makes 16 × 350 ml jars

1.5 kg japonicas (flowering quinces)
500 g cooking apples
10 cups water
juice of 1 lemon
sugar

Cut fruit in quarters. Put in a pan. Add water and lemon juice. Bring to boil slowly. Reduce heat. Simmer until fruit is very tender. Strain through jelly bag overnight. Next day sterilise the jars. Measure juice and return to pan. Add 1¾ cups of sugar to each 2 cups of juice. Dissolve sugar over low heat. Boil briskly until setting point is reached. Pack in hot jars, cover and let stand, then seal when cool.

MINT JELLY

Makes 3 × 250 ml jars

1 cup chopped mint leaves, firmly
  packed
3½ cups sugar
¾ cup water
¾ cup cider vinegar
½ cup pectin stock (see p. 10)

Put mint in pan with sugar, water and cider vinegar. Bring to boil. Stir until the sugar has dissolved. Boil gently for 3 minutes. Add pectin stock and boil hard for 1 minute. Strain through jelly bag. While straining, sterilise the jars. Pack strained juice into hot jars, cover, and seal when cool.

MINT AND APPLE JELLY

Makes 4 × 350 ml jars

---

1 kg cooking apples
water
sugar
10 sprigs mint
juice and rind of 1 lemon
½ cup wine vinegar
a few drops green food colouring

Roughly cut up apples. Put in pan. Cover with water and simmer until pulpy. Strain through jelly bag overnight. Next day sterilise the jars. Measure juice, return to the pan and add an equal quantity of sugar. Strip mint leaves from stalks, retain the leaves, and put the mint stalks and lemon rind in a muslin bag and add to pan. Add lemon juice and vinegar. Heat slowly to dissolve sugar, then add 3 tablespoons of chopped mint leaves, and food colouring as desired. Boil rapidly until set. Pour into hot jars, cover, and seal when cool.

> IN JELLY MAKING THERE IS NO NEED TO PEEL FRUIT SUCH AS APPLES OR TO REMOVE THE CORES. THESE ARE IMPORTANT IN GIVING FLAVOUR AND MAKING THE JELLY SET
>
> ▆
>
> TO CHOP PARSLEY QUICKLY, PUT A FEW SPRIGS IN A CUP AND SNIP WITH KITCHEN SCISSORS, TURNING THE CUP AS YOU CUT

MULBERRY JELLY

Makes 3 × 350 ml jars

---

500 g mulberries, stalks removed
1 large cooking apple, chopped
½ cup water
sugar

In a pan bring fruit and water to boil. Cover pan, reduce heat and simmer until pulpy. Strain through jelly bag overnight. Next day sterilise the jars. Measure juice and return to the pan. Add 1 cup of sugar to each cup of juice. Stir until dissolved. Boil briskly to setting point. Skim foam off surface. Put into hot jars, cover until cool, then seal.

PARSLEY JELLY

Makes 2 × 250 ml jars

---

100 g parsley, chopped
1 cup apple skins and cores
3 tablespoons lemon juice
1 teaspoon grated lemon rind
3 cups water
sugar

Put parsley, apple skins and cores, lemon juice, rind and water in a heavy pan. Bring to boil, then simmer for 30 minutes. Strain through a jelly bag overnight. Next day sterilise the jars. Measure juice and return to pan. Add ¾ cup of sugar to every cup of juice. Boil rapidly to setting point. Pack into hot jars, cover until cool, then seal.

PASSIONFRUIT JELLY

Makes 2 × 250 ml jars

---

24 passionfruit
3½ cups water
sugar

Put halved passionfruit in pan with water. Boil gently for 20 minutes. Strain, keeping liquid. Scoop pulp from passionfruit and place in pan with half the reserved liquid. Boil for 10 minutes. Strain through jelly bag overnight. Next day sterilise the jars. Measure juice and return to pan. Add ¾ cup of sugar to each cup of juice. Stir to dissolve, then boil to setting point. Pack and seal.

PINEAPPLE JELLY

Makes 2 × 250 ml jars

---

skin and core of 1 pineapple
1–2 cooking apples, chopped
juice and rind of 1–2 lemons
water
sugar

Roughly chop the pineapple skin and core. Put in pan with the apple (including core and peel) and lemon rind. (If the pineapple is large you will need 2 apples and lemons; if small, only use one.) Cover with cold water. Cover pan and boil for 45 minutes. Strain through a jelly bag overnight. Next day sterilise the jars. Measure

juice and return to pan. Add lemon juice and bring to the boil. Add ¾ cup of sugar to each 1 cup of liquid, stirring to dissolve. Boil briskly until setting point is reached. Pack in hot jars, cover, and seal when cool.

PLUM JELLY

Makes 4 × 250 ml jars

1.5 kg plums
3 cups water
sugar
3 tablespoons lemon juice

Wash and cut up plums. Put fruit and stones in pan. Cover with water and simmer until tender. Strain through a jelly bag overnight. Next day sterilise the jars. Measure juice and return to pan. Add 1 cup of sugar to each cup of juice. Heat slowly until sugar dissolves. Add lemon juice. Boil briskly until setting point is reached. Pack in hot jars, cover until cool, then seal.

PLUM AND BLACKBERRY JELLY

Makes 10 × 350 ml jars

1.8 kg plums
2 medium-sized lemons
7 cups water
2.2 kg blackberries
sugar

Slice each plum in three, leaving stones in fruit. Chop lemons roughly. Put in pan with plums and 4½ cups of the water. Simmer for 20 minutes. Add blackberries to pan with rest of water. Simmer for 25 minutes. Strain through jelly bag overnight. Next day sterilise the jars. Measure juice and add 200 g of sugar to each cup of juice. Stir to dissolve sugar. Boil rapidly to setting point. Pour into hot jars, cover until cool, then seal.

RED-CURRANT JELLY

Makes 4 × 250 ml jars

---

2 kg red currants
sugar

In a pan simmer the fruit very gently until the juice runs well. Strain overnight through a jelly bag. Next day sterilise the jars. Measure juice and return to the pan. Bring to boil and add ¾ cup of sugar to each cup of juice. Stir well until setting point is reached. Pour into hot jars and cover until cool, then seal.

ROSE GERANIUM JELLY

Makes 10 × 350 ml jars

2.7 kg crabapples
50 young rose geranium leaves
water
sugar

Wash, top and tail crabapples. Chop up, discarding bad parts. Put in pan with washed rose geranium leaves. Just cover with water. Simmer for 45 minutes, then drain through jelly bag overnight. Next day sterilise the jars. Measure juice and return to pan. Stir in 200 g of sugar to each cup of juice. Boil briskly for 10 minutes. Remove any scum. Pour into hot jars. Cover, and seal when cool.

ROWAN JELLY

Makes 4 × 350 ml jars

1.5 kg ripe rowanberries
water
sugar
juice of 1 lemon

Wash rowanberries. Remove stalks. Put in pan and just cover with water. Simmer until soft. Strain through jelly bag overnight. Next day sterilise the jars. Measure juice and return to pan. Add 200 g of sugar to each cup of juice. Add the lemon juice. Heat gently until sugar dissolves. Boil rapidly until setting point is reached. Pack in hot jars, cover until cool, then seal.

SWEET PEPPER JELLY

Makes 4 × 350 ml jars

---

500 g large red peppers
500 g large green peppers
2/3 cup cider vinegar
5 cups sugar
2/3 cup lemon juice
3/4 cup pectin stock (see p. 10)

Seed and core peppers. Put through blender to purée. Put in pan with vinegar and sugar. Stir until sugar is dissolved then bring to boil. Quickly turn off heat and let stand for 45 minutes. Stir in lemon juice. Boil briskly for 2 minutes. Stir in pectin stock. Strain through jelly bag overnight. Next day sterilise the jars. Skim the strained juice and pour into hot jars. Cover, and seal when cool.

WINE JELLY

Makes 5 × 350 ml jars

1.5 kg ripe green grapes
1 1/4 cups dry white wine
800 g cooking apples, sliced
1 lemon, thinly sliced
6 cardamom seeds
sugar
3/4 cup brandy

Put crushed grapes and wine in a pan. Bring to boil, then reduce heat and simmer until fruit is pulpy. Add apples, lemon and cardamom. Simmer until apples are pulpy. Strain through jelly bag overnight. Next day sterilise the jars. Measure liquid and return to pan. Stir in 400 g of sugar to each cup of juice. Add brandy. Boil briskly to setting point. Pour into hot jars, cover, and seal when cool.

MARMALADES

Marmalade is made from oranges, lemons, limes, grapefruit, tangerines, cumquats and tangelos, alone or in various combinations. Though the citrus taste must predominate, various flavourings may be added, such as apricot, brandy, carrot, ginger, treacle or whisky. Marmalade making is similar to jam making but, as marmalade contains rind, longer cooking is needed and more water required. It is simmered until the rind is soft, and the amount of liquid is reduced by half. About 500 g of fruit is used to make 1.5 kg of marmalade. Jelly marmalades are strained through a jelly bag after the fruit has been pulped. Strips of rind are then added.

Scrub the fruit thoroughly if it is at all dirty. Halve the fruit. Squeeze out the juice and reserve. Reserve the pips. Remove the white pith from the rind and discard. Roughly chop the rind and tie it in a muslin bag with the pips. For a medium-thick marmalade, the rind can be finely shredded and cooked with the fruit. To make a chunkier, thicker marmalade, leave all or part of the pith on the rind, and prepare it in a mincer or food processor. Simmer fruit, juice, rind, and pips in muslin bag until rind is soft (about 2 hours).

The pectin is contained in the pips and the white pith of citrus fruit, not in the rind as is generally supposed. Extra acid (lemon juice) is sometimes added to ensure a good set. When a pectin test (see p. 10) proves satisfactory, measure the fruit pulp in the pan. Add 1 cup of sugar to each cup of pulp.

After the sugar has dissolved, marmalade must be briskly boiled to reach the setting point quickly. More than 20 minutes boiling time darkens marmalade and spoils its flavour. The setting test is as for jam (see p. 11). Marmalade is usually allowed to cool slightly before packing (if unnecessary, the recipe omits this instruction), as this ensures the fruit will be well distributed in the jars.

APRICOT MARMALADE

Makes 14 × 350 ml jars

---

500 g dried apricots
500 g sweet oranges
500 g lemons
14 cups water
3 kg sugar

First sterilise the jars. Wash fruit. Cut oranges and lemons in half and squeeze out juice. Tie pips in a muslin bag. Discard pith. Shred the orange and lemon rind and chop the apricots. Put apricots, rind, juice, muslin bag and water in a heavy based pan. Bring to boil. Simmer until fruit and rind are soft. Remove the muslin bag. Stir in the sugar to dissolve. Boil to setting point. Stand for 10 minutes. Pour into hot jars, cover until cool, then seal.

APRICOT AND MANDARIN MARMALADE

Makes 6 × 350 ml jars

---

4 mandarins
1 lemon
2 cups boiling water
250 g dried apricots
3 cups cold water
sugar

Take rind from mandarins and lemon, discarding white pith. Shred rind. Put mandarin and lemon pulp in a non-metallic bowl and add boiling water. Put apricots in a bowl with cold water. Let both stand overnight. Next day sterilise the jars. Combine contents of both bowls in a heavy pan with rind. Simmer until fruit is soft. Measure mixture and return to the pan. Add 1 cup of sugar to each cup of pulp. Boil to setting point. Pack in hot jars, cover until cool and seal.

CARROT MARMALADE

Makes 6 × 350 ml jars

---

500 g carrots
2 lemons
2 oranges
5 cups water
8 cups sugar

Peel carrots and grate them. Wash lemons and oranges. Slice finely. Put carrots and fruit in non-metallic bowl. Add water and let stand overnight. Next day sterilise the jars, then transfer contents of bowl to a pan. Cook until rinds are soft. Stir in sugar to dissolve. Boil briskly until setting point is reached. Allow to cool slightly before packing into hot jars. Cover until cool, then seal.

WHEN USING THE RIND OF A LEMON, ORANGE OR GRAPEFRUIT, TAKE CARE NOT TO USE THE PITH BECAUSE IT WILL GIVE A BITTER TASTE

MIXED CITRUS FRUIT MARMALADE

Makes 7 × 350 ml jars

1 kg mixed citrus fruits
7 cups cold water
sugar

First sterilise the jars. Halve fruit. Squeeze juice. Put the seeds and roughly cut white pith in a muslin bag. Put juice, flesh and bag in a pan with water. Simmer until reduced by half. Remove bag. Measure pulp and return to the pan. Add 1 cup of sugar to each cup of pulp, stirring until dissolved, then boil briskly to setting point. Skim froth. Let stand for a few minutes, then stir to distribute fruit. Pour into hot jars. Cover, and seal when cool.

CITRUS SKIN MARMALADE

Makes 3 × 350 ml jars

500 g citrus skins
½ cup lemon juice
5 cups water
6 cups sugar

The skins for this recipe can be fresh or defrosted from frozen (lemon juice is used in many jam recipes, and you can freeze any left-over skins for this marmalade). Wash skins. Put through blender. Put in non-metallic bowl with lemon juice and water. Let stand overnight. Next day sterilise the jars. Then transfer contents of bowl to a heavy pan and boil gently until skins are soft. Stir in sugar until it is dissolved. Boil briskly until setting point is reached. Leave to cool a little, then stir to distribute fruit. Pack in hot jars, cover until cool and seal.

CUMQUAT MARMALADE

Makes 4 × 350 ml jars

1.5 kg cumquats
8 cups water
sugar

Finely shred washed rind. Tie in muslin bag. Squeeze juice from fruit and set aside. Roughly chop up flesh. Put in non-metallic bowl with water and muslin bag. Let stand overnight. Next day sterilise the jars. Transfer contents of bowl to pan and add juice. Simmer until soft. Retain bag of rinds. Strain through jelly bag. Measure juice. Return juice to pan and stir in rinds and 1 cup of sugar to each cup of liquid. When sugar is dissolved, boil briskly to setting point. Pour into hot jars, cover until cool, then seal.

DUNDEE MARMALADE

Makes 8 × 350 ml jars

1.5 kg Seville oranges
2 lemons
6 cups water
12 cups sugar

First sterilise the jars. Put whole, washed fruit in pan with the water. Cover. Simmer until fruit is soft. Lift out of water, cool and chop up. Tie seeds in muslin bag. Put bag in liquid. Boil for 5 minutes. Remove bag and squeeze it. Add fruit to liquid in the pan. Stir in sugar until it dissolves. Rapidly boil until setting point is reached. Cool slightly, then pack in hot jars and seal when cold.

FIVE-FRUIT MARMALADE

Makes 5 × 350 ml jars

---

1 orange
1 lemon
1 grapefruit
1 large cooking apple
1 cooking pear
5 cups water
6 cups sugar

Sterilise the jars. Wash all fruit and cut in half. Strain citrus juice into pan. Peel and core apple and pear, tie peels and cores in a bag with citrus pips and half the pith. Cut up citrus rind and membrane. Add to pan with bag and water. Simmer until rind is soft. Squeeze bag and discard it. Stir in sugar until it is dissolved. Boil briskly until setting point is reached. Cool slightly and stir to distribute fruit before packing in hot jars, cover until cool, then seal.

THREE-FRUIT MARMALADE

Makes 5 × 350 ml jars

---

1 medium-sized grapefruit
2 lemons
1 sweet orange
6 cups water
1.25 kg sugar

Cut washed fruit in half. Squeeze out juice. Put pips in muslin bag. Peel and finely shred rinds. Put in a non-metallic bowl with juice, muslin bag and water. Cover and let stand overnight. Next day sterilise the jars. Transfer contents of bowl to a pan and simmer until soft. Discard bag. Stir in sugar until it dissolves. Boil briskly to setting point. Cool a little, then stir to distribute fruit. Pack in hot jars, cover, and seal when cool.

AVOID BOILING FRUIT TOO QUICKLY TO SOFTEN IT OR TOO SLOWLY ONCE THE SUGAR HAS DISSOLVED

GINGER MARMALADE

Makes 4 × 350 ml jars

---

500 g grapefruit
150 g lemons
100 g peeled root ginger
6 cups water
sugar

First sterilise the jars. Cut fruit in half. Squeeze juice and strain. Tie seeds in muslin bag. Put citrus skins and ginger through mincer. Put all fruit, water, juice and bag of seeds in pan. Cover. Simmer until soft. Discard bag of seeds and measure pulp. Return to pan and stir in 1 cup of sugar to each cup of juice. Briskly boil until setting point is reached. Pack in hot jars, cover until cool, then seal.

GRAPEFRUIT MARMALADE

Makes 12 × 350 ml jars

---

1 kg grapefruit
500 g lemons
14 cups water
3 kg sugar

Sterilise the jars. Finely shred the rinds of the washed fruit. Tie white pith and pips in muslin bag. Chop fruit flesh. Put in pan with rind, bag and water. Simmer until tender. Discard bag. Stir in sugar until it dissolves. Boil briskly until setting point is reached. Remove scum and let cool a little. Stir before pouring into hot jars. Cover until cool, then seal.

JELLY SHRED MARMALADE

Makes 4 × 350 ml jars

1.5 kg citrus fruit
8 cups water
sugar

Finely shred yellow rind and tie in muslin bag. Squeeze juice from fruit. Roughly chop flesh and pith. Put in non-metallic bowl with pips, water and bag of rind. Let stand overnight. Next day sterilise the jars, then transfer contents of bowl to pan and simmer until soft. Strain through a jelly bag. Retain bag of rind. Measure juice and return to pan. Add rinds from the bag and 1 cup of sugar to each cup of juice. Stir to dissolve sugar, then boil briskly to setting point. Pour into hot jars, cover until cool and then seal.

LEMON MARMALADE

Makes 8 × 350 ml jars

8 ripe lemons
10 cups cold water
sugar

First sterilise the jars. Finely shred yellow rind. Finely chop flesh. Tie seeds and white pith in muslin bag. Put flesh, rind and bag in pan with water. Simmer until reduced by half. Discard bag. Measure pulp and return to the pan. Add 1 cup of sugar to 1 cup of pulp, stirring to dissolve. Boil briskly to setting point. Skim off scummy foam. Let stand briefly, then stir before packing to distribute fruit. Cover until cold, then seal.

LEMON JELLY MARMALADE

Makes 6 × 350 ml jars

1 kg lemons
10 cups water
sugar

First sterilise the jars. Finely shred the yellow lemon rind. Squeeze and strain juice. Save shells. Tie shells and pips in a bag, and put with the lemon rind, juice and water in a heavy pan. Simmer until soft. Discard bag. Strain liquid through jelly bag. Measure juice and return to pan. Stir in ¾ cup of sugar to 1 cup of liquid. Boil briskly to setting point. Pour into hot jars, cover, cool, and seal.

LIME MARMALADE

Makes 7 × 350 ml jars

10 medium-sized ripe limes
10 cups cold water
sugar

First sterilise the jars. Shred rinds finely. Discard pips. Tie white pith in muslin bag. Chop flesh finely, reserving juice. Put flesh, water, juice, rind and bag in pan. Simmer until reduced by half. Discard bag. Measure pulp and return to the pan. Stir in 1 cup of sugar to 1 cup of pulp. Boil briskly until setting point is reached. Skim off scum. Stir to distribute fruit, then pack, cover, and seal when cool.

MANDARIN MARMALADE

Makes 6 × 350 ml jars

450 g mandarins
450 g grapefruit
12 cups water
sugar

Slice or coarsely grate fruit skins. Squeeze juice and set aside. Tie pips in a muslin bag. Put in a non-metallic bowl with water and skins and let stand overnight. Next day sterilise the jars, then transfer contents of bowl to pan and add juice. Simmer until the rind is soft. Discard bag. Measure pulp and return to the pan. Stir in 1 cup of sugar to each cup of pulp. Boil to setting point. Pour into hot jars, cover, and seal when cool.

MINT AND LEMON MARMALADE

Makes 8 × 350 ml jars

8 medium-sized lemons
4½ cups water
7¼ cups sugar
8 tablespoons freshly chopped mint
  leaves

Halve lemons and squeeze them. Remove rind and chop it according to the marmalade texture required. Put strained lemon juice, water and strips of rind in a non-metallic bowl. Add pips tied in a muslin bag. Cover and let stand overnight. Next day, sterilise jars, then transfer contents of bowl to a pan and simmer for 1 hour. Remove bag from pan. Stir in sugar until dissolved. Boil briskly for 10 minutes, then let cool. Stir in mint. Pack in hot jars, cover, and seal when cool.

OLD-FASHIONED SWEET MARMALADE

Makes 4 × 350 ml jars

500 g sweet oranges
150 g lemons
7 cups water
1 tablespoon treacle
sugar

First sterilise the jars. Cut washed fruit in half. Squeeze juice. Finely slice rind. Tie pips in a muslin bag. Put water, juice, rind and bag in pan. Cover and simmer until tender. Discard bag. Measure pulp and return to the pan. Add treacle and then stir in 1 cup of sugar to each cup of pulp until it dissolves. Boil briskly to setting point. Pack in hot jars, cover, cool and then seal.

BITTER ORANGE MARMALADE

Makes 7 × 350 ml jars

500 g Seville oranges
juice of 1 lemon
5 cups cold water
sugar

First sterilise the jars. Wash the oranges, halve them and squeeze out the juice and reserve. Reserve the pips. Remove the white pith from the rind, roughly chop rind and tie in a muslin bag with the pips. Put orange pulp and juice and muslin bag in a heavy pan. Add lemon juice and water. Simmer until liquid is reduced by half. Test for pectin and if satisfactory remove muslin bag. Measure pulp, return to the pan, and add 1 cup of sugar to each cup of pulp. Heat gently and stir until it dissolves. Boil rapidly until setting point is reached. Pour into hot jars, cover until cool and seal.

DARK SEVILLE ORANGE MARMALADE

Makes 11 × 350 ml jars

1.5 kg Seville oranges
2 lemons
17 cups water
3 kg soft dark brown sugar
2 tablespoons molasses

Sterilise the jars. Put whole, washed fruits in pan with water. Cover. Simmer until the fruit is soft (about 10–15 minutes). Lift out of water (but reserve water in pan) and chop. Tie the pips in a muslin bag. Boil pips in pan for 5 minutes. Squeeze out bag and discard. Add fruit to pan. Stir in sugar and molasses. Boil rapidly to setting point. Cool, pack, and cover. Seal when cold.

ORANGE JELLY MARMALADE

Makes 8 × 350 ml jars

1 kg Seville oranges
1 lemon
10 cups cold water
8 cups sugar

Halve fruit. Squeeze juice into pan. Finely cut rind. Tie rind in a muslin bag with pips and pith. Put in pan. Add water. Simmer for 2 hours. Remove bag, reserve it, and strain liquid through jelly bag overnight. Next day sterilise the jars. Measure liquid and return to pan. Add 1 cup of sugar to each cup of liquid, and rind from muslin bag. Boil rapidly to the setting point. Cool slightly, stir to distribute fruit, then pack in hot jars, cover, and seal when cool.

ORANGE AND PEACH MARMALADE

Makes 12 × 350 ml jars

4 thin-skinned oranges
juice of 1 lemon
4 cups water
4 peaches
3 cups sugar

Sterilise the jars. Remove pips from oranges and tie in muslin bag. Finely mince oranges and skins. Put in pan with water, lemon juice and bag. Simmer until soft. Skin, stone and slice peaches. Add to orange mixture in pan. Cook for 5 minutes. Remove bag. Measure pulp and return to the pan. Add ¾ cup of sugar to each cup of pulp, and stir until dissolved. Boil briskly to setting point. Skim. Pack in hot jars. Cover until cool, then seal.

PINEAPPLE AND RUM MARMALADE

Makes 4 × 350 ml jars

1 orange
water
3 cups finely chopped fresh pineapple
   flesh
2½ cups sugar
¼ cup dark rum

Peel orange and finely shred rind (discard pith). Cover with water in a non-metallic bowl. Finely chop up the orange flesh and add to pineapple in a separate bowl. Mix in the sugar. Stand overnight. Next day, sterilise the jars, transfer rind and water to pan and boil for 5 minutes, and then add the orange and pineapple mixture. Boil briskly to set. Mix in rum. Pour into hot jars, cover, and seal when cool.

QUINCE MARMALADE

Makes 6 × 350 ml jars

1.5 kg quinces
5 lemons
5 cups water
6 cups sugar

Sterilise the jars. Wash, peel, core and grate quinces. Grate rind from lemons, halve them and squeeze juice and reserve it. Tie the quince peel, cores, seeds and lemon shells in a muslin bag. Put in a heavy pan with water, lemon rind and quince flesh. Simmer until tender. Discard bag. Add 6 tablespoons of the reserved lemon juice and stir in the sugar until it has dissolved. Boil rapidly to setting point. Remove from heat and allow to cool slightly before packing.

TANGERINE MARMALADE

Makes 12 × 350 ml jars

1 kg tangerines
500 g lemons
14 cups water
2.5 kg sugar

Sterilise the jars. Cut fruit in half. Squeeze out juice. Tie pips in muslin bag. Peel and shred rinds and put in pan with the water, juice and muslin bag. Simmer until rinds are tender. Discard muslin bag. Stir in sugar until dissolved. Boil briskly until setting point is reached. Remove any scum. Cool slightly. Pour into hot jars. Cover, and seal when cool.

TOMATO MARMALADE

Makes 5 × 350 ml jars

1.5 kg firm, ripe tomatoes
grated rind of 1 lemon
juice of 3 lemons
1.5 kg sugar

Sterilise the jars. Skin and slice tomatoes. (Tomatoes skin easily after immersion in boiling water for 30 seconds.) Simmer tomatoes, rind and juice in a pan until rind is soft. Stir in sugar until it is dissolved. Boil briskly until setting point is reached. Pour into hot jars. Cover, and seal when cold.

TROPICAL MARMALADE

Makes 4 × 350 ml jars

---

250 g grapefruit
100 g lemon
100 g orange
1 small pineapple
4 cups water
sugar

Sterilise the jars. Finely shred yellow rind of citrus fruits. Chop white pith. Put pith in a muslin bag with pips. Peel and chop pineapple, catching all juice possible. Put fruit, rind, juices, muslin bag and water in pan. Boil until tender. Discard bag. Measure pulp and return to the pan. Stir in 1 cup of sugar to each cup of pulp. Boil to setting point. Allow to stand, before packing.

WHISKY MARMALADE

Makes 5 × 350 ml jars

---

6 sweet oranges
2 lemons
6 cups water
5 cups sugar
½ cup whisky

The total weight of the fruit should be 1.4–1.5 kg. Cut washed fruit in quarters, then cut in thin slices. Put in non-metallic bowl with water. Let stand overnight. Next day sterilise the jars. Transfer contents of bowl to a heavy pan. Simmer until tender. Stir in sugar until dissolved. Boil, uncovered, to setting point. Add the whisky and stir in well. Remove from heat. Cool a little. Pack and seal when cool.

$\mathcal{M}$ICROWAVE PRESERVES

Microwave preserve making is very fast (about 15 minutes, depending on the fruit) and the jam, jelly or marmalade will not scorch, unlike that cooked on a conventional stove top. The preserves do not need constant stirring, but they do require some attention so it is necessary to remain in the kitchen while microwaving.

The jars must be hot and sterilised. This should be done in a conventional oven as the microwave does not give the necessary constant high heat.

Choose ripe fruits at the peak of maturity, as fruit that is less ripe will not impart sufficient sweetness to the preserve. Most fruits need to be chopped, and though this can be done in a food processor it is better done by hand. This produces a more uniform size – an important necessity to ensure even cooking in a microwave oven.

In a microwave there is a danger of boil-over unless the container used is generously oversized. The most suitable is a 2-litre glass measure that has a lip or a spout that facilitates pouring the hot, bubbling mixture into hot jars. The jars are not completely filled as microwave preserves bubble furiously when they are cooked and tend to spill over the rims of the jars.

Here is a selection of jams, jellies and marmalades suitable for microwaving. Do not double the recipes or alter the quantities in any way, for the relationships of quantity, size of container and timing are crucial.

Fruits can be prepared and mixed with the sugar and flavourings mentioned in the recipes, and then deep-frozen. Later a portion may be thawed out and cooked by following the recipes.

APPLE JAM

Makes 5 × 300 ml jars

4–5 cooking apples
1½ cups sugar
½ teaspoon butter
1 tablespoon lemon juice
1 teaspoon ground cinnamon

Sterilise the jars. Peel, core and dice apples. Place 2 cups of apple in a 2–3 litre container. Add the sugar, butter, lemon and cinnamon. Stir well. Cover. Cook on HIGH (100% power) for 6 minutes, until the mixture boils. Remove cover and stir. Cook, uncovered, on HIGH for 5–7 minutes. Test on a saucer for consistency. Pour into hot jars until two-thirds full. Cover until cool, then seal.

APRICOT JAM

Makes 5 × 300 ml jars

---

2 cups diced apricots
2 tablespoons lemon juice
1½ cups sugar
½ teaspoon butter

Sterilise the jars. Place all ingredients in a 2–3 litre container. Stir well. Cover. Cook on HIGH (100% power) for 6 minutes until mixture boils. Remove cover and stir fruit mixture. Cook, uncovered, on HIGH for 10–12 minutes. Test on saucer for setting consistency. Pour into hot jars until two-thirds full. Cover, and seal when cool.

APRICOT AND PINEAPPLE JAM

Makes 5 × 300 ml jars

1½ cups diced apricots
½ cup canned unsweetened crushed
  pineapple
1 tablespoon lemon juice
1½ cups sugar
½ teaspoon butter

Sterilise the jars. Place all ingredients in a 2–3 litre container. Stir well. Cover. Microwave on HIGH (100% power) for 6 minutes or until mixture boils. Remove cover and stir fruit mixture. Cook, uncovered, on HIGH for 13–15 minutes. Test on saucer for setting consistency. Pour into hot jars until two-thirds full. Cover, and seal when cool.

BERRY JAM

Makes 5 × 300 ml jars

---

2 cups crushed blackberries or
  boysenberries or raspberries
1 tablespoon lemon juice
1½ cups sugar
½ teaspoon butter

Sterilise the jars. Place all ingredients in a 2–3 litre container. Stir well. Cover. Microwave on HIGH (100% power) for 6 minutes or until mixture boils. Remove cover and stir fruit mixture. Cook, uncovered, on HIGH for 13–15 minutes. Test on saucer for setting consistency. Pour into hot jars until two-thirds full. Cover, and seal when cool.

BLUEBERRY JAM

Makes 5 × 300 ml jars

2 cups crushed blueberries
1 tablespoon lemon juice
1½ cups sugar
½ teaspoon butter

Sterilise the jars. Place ingredients in a 2–3 litre container. Stir thoroughly and cover. Cook on HIGH (100% power) for 6 minutes or until it starts to boil. Remove cover and stir mixture. Cook, uncovered, on HIGH for 9–11 minutes. Test on saucer for setting consistency. Pour into hot jars until two-thirds full. Cover, and seal when cool.

CHERRY JAM

Makes 5 × 300 ml jars

2 cups halved and stoned cherries
¼ cup lemon juice
½ teaspoon ground cinnamon
1½ cups sugar
½ teaspoon butter

Sterilise the jars. Place ingredients in a 2–3 litre container. Stir thoroughly and cover. Cook on HIGH (100% power) for 6 minutes or until it starts to boil. Remove cover and stir mixture. Cook,

uncovered, on HIGH for 9–11 minutes. Test on saucer for setting consistency. Pour into hot jars until two-thirds full. Cover, and seal when cool.

FIG AND ORANGE JAM

Makes 5 × 300 ml jars

1½ cups diced figs
½ cup chopped orange flesh
1½ teaspoons grated orange rind
3 tablespoons lemon juice
¼ teaspoon ground cloves
¼ teaspoon ground ginger
¼ teaspoon ground cinnamon

Sterilise the jars. Place ingredients in a 2–3 litre container. Stir thoroughly and cover. Cook on HIGH (100% power) for 6 minutes or until it starts to boil. Remove cover and stir mixture. Cook, uncovered, on HIGH for 13–15 minutes. Test on a saucer for setting consistency. Pour into hot jars until two-thirds full. Cover, and seal when cool.

AVOID USING JARS THAT ARE NOT PERFECT. THEY MAY BREAK WHEN A HOT PRESERVE IS POURED INTO THEM

DON'T FORGET TO LABEL AND DATE YOUR PRESERVES

PEACH OR NECTARINE JAM

Makes 5 × 300 ml jars

2 cups peeled and chopped peaches or
   nectarines
1 tablespoon lemon juice
1½ cups sugar
½ teaspoon butter
2 drops almond essence

Sterilise the jars. Place all ingredients except almond essence in a 2–3 litre container. Stir thoroughly and cover. Cook on HIGH (100% power) for 6 minutes or until it starts to boil. Remove cover and stir mixture. Cook, uncovered, on HIGH for 13–15 minutes. Test for setting point on saucer. Add almond essence. Pour into hot jars until two-thirds full. Cover, and seal when cool.

STRAWBERRY JAM

Makes 5 × 300 ml jars

3½ cups hulled strawberries
1½ tablespoons lemon juice
1½ cups sugar
½ teaspoon butter

Sterilise the jars. Crush strawberries to make 2 cups. Add the lemon juice. Place in large container. Add sugar and butter. Mix thoroughly. Cover. Microwave on HIGH (100% power) until it comes to boil. Remove cover and stir.

Microwave, uncovered, on HIGH for 15–20 minutes. Pour into hot jars. Cover and let cool before sealing.

QUINCE JELLY

Makes 5 × 300 ml jars

1.5 kg washed, unripe quinces
hot water
sugar
175 g peeled root ginger, chopped if
   necessary
juice and pared rind of 1 lemon

Sterilise the jars. Cut quinces into small pieces. Place in a large bowl. Barely cover with hot water. Cover bowl. Cook about 13–15 minutes until tender on HIGH (100% power). Strain through jelly bag. Measure liquid and return to the bowl. Add 450 g of sugar to each 2 cups of liquid. Stir until dissolved. Add ginger, lemon rind (keep it in large pieces to facilitate removal later) and lemon juice. Cook, uncovered, on HIGH about 5–7 minutes, until setting point is reached. Test for setting consistency on saucer. Remove ginger and rind. Pour into hot jars until two-thirds full. Cover and let cool, then seal.

> **AVOID PRESSING PRESERVES THROUGH THE JELLY BAG TO SAVE TIME. YOU WILL END UP WITH A CLOUDY JELLY**

SWEET ORANGE MARMALADE

Makes 8 × 350 ml jars

5 large oranges
juice of 2 lemons
3½ cups boiling water
1.8 kg sugar

Sterilise the jars. Squeeze juice from fruit. Place orange and lemon juice in a large 4-litre bowl. Cut orange rind from pith and tie pith and pips in a muslin bag. Add to bowl. Finely shred orange rind. Add to bowl with the boiling water. Cover. Cook on HIGH (100% power) for 25–30 minutes, stirring once. Remove bag, add sugar and stir well. Cook, uncovered, for 20–25 minutes on HIGH, stirring every 5 minutes. Test for consistency on saucer. Pot, cover, and seal when cool.

PUMPKIN MARMALADE

Makes 5 × 300 ml jars

900 g peeled and deseeded pumpkin
900 g sugar
2 oranges, thinly sliced

Cut pumpkin into small cubes. Layer with sugar and let stand for 8 hours in a non-metallic bowl, covered. Sterilise the jars. Add the sliced oranges to the pumpkin. Cook, uncovered, in a large container for 45–50 minutes on SIMMER (40% power), stirring every 5 minutes until setting point is reached. Pour into hot jars. Cover and let cool, then seal.

DIABETIC PRESERVES

Commercial diabetic jams and marmalades are not entirely suitable for persons with diabetes, according to a report from Dr Allan Borushek of Western Australia, who is an active member of the Western Australian Diabetic Association and of the Nutrition Society of Australia. Dr Borushek is a consultant to the food industry, and other private groups. He believes that the use of sorbital and glycerine in commercial diabetic jams in place of sugar is of no advantage. Sorbital and glycerine are converted to sugar in the body and there is no subsequent saving in calories. So here are some recipes using Sugarine instead.

DIABETIC APPLE JELLY

Makes 2 × 250 ml jars

1.75 kg cooking apples
7 cups cold water
Sugarine

Sterilise the jars. Chop the apples, discarding any bruised parts. Put the apple in a pan with the water. Bring to the boil, then simmer until the fruit is very soft. Mash and strain through a jelly bag. Test the liquid for pectin and measure the juice and return it to the pan. Heat gently, then stir in 2 teaspoons of Sugarine to each cup of juice. Boil rapidly until it reaches the setting point. Remove the scum. Pack in hot jars and seal.

DIABETIC GRAPEFRUIT MARMALADE

Makes 2 × 250 ml jars

---

500 g grapefruit
250 g lemons
¾ cup water
4 tablespoons Sugarine

Sterilise the jars. Wash the fruit. Peel the yellow rind very finely. Remove the white pith and tie in a muslin bag with the pips. Finely shred the yellow rind. Chop the fleshy part of the fruit. Put it in a pan with the water, rind and the muslin bag of pips and pith. Simmer until the rind is tender, then boil briskly for about 25 minutes. Stir in the Sugarine. Let the mixture cool a little. Stir again. Pack into hot jars and seal.

DIABETIC MARMALADE

Makes 2 × 350 ml jars

---

4 large oranges
2 cups boiling water
2 tablespoons Sugarine
1 cup pectin stock (see p. 10)

Sterilise the jars. Wash and dry the oranges. Drop in hot water, or microwave, for 2 minutes, then squeeze the juice into a bowl. Discard the pith and the pips. Finely shred the rind and add to the juice in the bowl. Add the boiling water, and transfer juice, rind and water to a pan. Boil, uncovered, for 20 minutes. Add the Sugarine and stir while cooking for 5 minutes more. Remove from the heat. Add pectin. Let stand for 10 minutes, pack in hot jars and seal.

DIABETIC CUCUMBER PICKLES

Makes 2 × 300 ml jars

6 cucumbers
¼ cup salt
2 cups white vinegar
¼ cup water
2 tablespoons whole pickling spices
1½ teaspoons Sugarine

Wash and dry the cucumbers and cut into 10-cm strips. Place in a non-metallic bowl. Sprinkle with salt. Allow to stand overnight. Next day, sterilise the jars, rinse cucumber and drain thoroughly. Put the vinegar and water in a pan and bring to the boil. Tie the pickling spices in a muslin bag and add to the pan. Add the cucumbers and Sugarine. Reduce the heat and simmer for about 15 minutes. Put the cucumbers in hot jars. Heat the liquid again to boiling point, and pour over the cucumbers in the jars. Seal immediately.

DON'T FORGET TO LABEL AND DATE YOUR PRESERVES

DO NOT USE COPPER, IRON OR BRASS PANS WHEN MAKING CHUTNEYS, RELISHES, PICKLES AND SAUCES

DON'T USE METALLIC TOPS FOR SEALING ANY PRESERVE CONTAINING VINEGAR

DIABETIC CHILLI SAUCE

Makes 10 × 250 ml jars

8 cups peeled and chopped tomatoes
¼ cup chopped green peppers
½ cup chopped red peppers
1½ cups chopped onion
1½ cups chopped celery
1½ cups cider vinegar
1 tablespoon salt
1 teaspoon soy sauce
1 tablespoon Tabasco sauce
1 cinnamon stick
1 teaspoon cloves
1½ teaspoons celery seeds
1½ teaspoons mustard seeds
1 teaspoon Sugarine

In a pan put tomatoes, peppers, onion, celery, vinegar, salt, soy and Tabasco sauces. Put all the spices in a muslin bag and add to the pan. Bring to the boil, then reduce the heat and simmer gently for about 5–6 hours, stirring occasionally. Meanwhile sterilise jars. When sauce is cooked, remove the bag of spices. Allow to cool a little, then stir in the Sugarine. Let stand for 10 minutes. Stir again. Pack into hot jars and seal immediately.

CHUTNEYS

Chutney is a pungent, spicy condiment, produced from fruits and vegetables cooked in vinegar, which acts as the preservative. It may be sweet or hot, and can be made from almost any type of fruit or vegetable. The produce should be ripe, but not over-ripe. Damaged areas should be discarded, but diseased fruit or vegetables should never be used. When the recipe calls for cucumbers, and they have ripened to the stage where the seeds have hardened, these may be scraped out and discarded.

The sweetened mixture is thick, and has an even texture – not unlike jam – but without the jellied quality. The fruit and vegetables should be cooked slowly for a long time to ensure an even, mellow taste. Don't use copper, brass, iron or chipped enamel pans – these will impart an unpleasant taste and poor colour.

The fruit and vegetables should be peeled, then cored, seeded or stoned, according to type. Then they may be coarsely minced, chopped small or sliced. The sugar, flavourings and vinegar are added and the whole cooked until soft. Malt vinegar (of good quality – either white or brown as the colour of the chutney is determined by the cooked fruit) is usually used in making chutney. Brown sugar and golden syrup can be used to give a darker colour, and also to vary the flavour.

To add flavour to chutney use dried fruits such as dates, prunes, raisins and crystallised ginger. Cook with the lid off and stir frequently, especially during the latter stages. Tasting chutney while still warm will give a very false idea of the flavour, which may seem too spicy or too hot. The chutney's flavour will mellow with storage.

Chutney should be packed while still hot. If using metal lids, a wax liner should be put between the product and the lid to avoid tainting by the metal, as the vinegar will make the metal corrode. Plastic lids are preferable to metal for this reason.

Chutney generally improves with maturity, and will store very well if kept in a cool, dark place. Chutney – and also relish – should be stored for at least 6 to 8 weeks before using, to allow the flavours to develop and mature. Once a jar of chutney has been opened, it should be kept in the refrigerator.

PROBLEMS AND REMEDIES

SHRINKING AND DRYING OUT
This is caused by storage conditions being too warm, or poor covering of the jar allowing some evaporation of moisture. Remove the dry part and use remainder.

MOULD
This can occur if jars or lids are not perfectly clean or if the storage area is too damp. Remove the mould and the layer beneath. Use the remainder.

SYRUPY LIQUID ON TOP
This is due to insufficient cooking time, or cooking with the saucepan lid on, resulting in the moisture not evaporating sufficiently. The storage time will be limited, so use the chutney before too long.

DISCOLOURATION
This is caused by using the wrong type of pan. Do not use copper, iron, brass or chipped enamel utensils. Chutney made in these pans will have an unpleasant taste. Nothing can be done.

APPLE CHUTNEY

Makes 6 × 350 ml jars

---

1 kg cooking apples
2 cups raisins
2 cups brown sugar
1 teaspoon salt
¼ teaspoon cayenne pepper
1-cm piece peeled root ginger
1 tablespoon mustard seeds
3 cups malt vinegar

Sterilise the jars. Peel, core and chop apples. Put in a pan with raisins, sugar, salt and cayenne pepper. Crush the ginger. Tie in a muslin bag with the mustard seeds. Add to pan and pour in vinegar. Bring the mixture to the boil and simmer gently, stirring frequently, uncovered, for about 1 hour. Pack into hot jars, cover, and seal when cool.

APPLE AND DATE CHUTNEY

Makes 6 × 350 ml jars

---

1 kg cooking apples
450 g onions
450 g stoned dates
275 g raw sugar
1 teaspoon mustard powder
½ teaspoon turmeric
½ teaspoon ground ginger
2⅓ cups malt vinegar

Sterilise the jars. Peel, core and slice the apples. Chop up the onions, and finely chop the dates.

Put all these ingredients together in a pan. Add the sugar, mustard, turmeric, ginger and vinegar. Bring slowly to the boil, stirring until the sugar has dissolved. Reduce the heat and simmer, uncovered, for about 45 minutes, stirring frequently to avoid burning. Pack into hot jars, cover, and seal when cool.

HOT APPLE AND MARROW CHUTNEY

Makes 8 × 350 ml jars

---

2 kg cooking apples
1 kg marrow
500 g onions
1 kg sugar
6 cups malt vinegar
250 g currants
250 g raisins
75 g salt
3 tablespoons ground ginger
3 tablespoons mustard powder
1 tablespoon turmeric
5 red chillies, chopped
a few blades mace

Peel, core and chop apples. Peel, deseed and chop marrow. Peel and chop up onions. Mix all the ingredients in a large non-metallic bowl and leave to stand overnight. Next day sterilise the jars, then transfer contents of the bowl to a pan and heat slowly to the boil. Simmer for 2 hours, uncovered, until a rich brown colour, stirring occasionally. Pack into hot jars, cover, and seal when cool.

APPLE AND MINT CHUTNEY

Makes 2 × 350 ml jars

---

450 g cooking apples
3 onions
1/2 cup roughly chopped mint
1 2/3 cups vinegar
1 cup brown sugar
3/4 cup raisins
1 teaspoon mustard powder
1/2 teaspoon chilli powder
1 teaspoon salt

First sterilise the jars. Peel and chop apples and onions. Put apples, onions and mint in pan with the vinegar, sugar, raisins, mustard, chilli powder and salt. Heat, stirring, until boiling point is reached. Stirring occasionally, simmer for about 1½ hours, uncovered. Pack in hot jars, cover, and seal when cool.

APRICOT CHUTNEY

Makes 2 × 350 ml jars

---

450 g dried apricots
450 g onions
225 g sugar
2 1/3 cups cider vinegar
1/2 teaspoon turmeric
1 teaspoon mustard powder
2 cloves garlic, crushed

Sterilise the jars. Chop apricots and onions. Place in a pan with all the other ingredients. Stir well and let stand for 2 hours. Gently heat, stirring until sugar dissolves. Bring to boil, then reduce heat, cover and simmer for 2 hours. Stir frequently to prevent sticking. Pack, cover, and seal when cool.

APRICOT GOTHIC CHUTNEY

Makes 2 × 350 ml jars

---

2 1/3 cups malt vinegar
250 g brown sugar
500 g dried apricots
3-cm piece root ginger (optional)
2 cinnamon sticks
6 peppercorns
4 whole allspice
1/2 teaspoon mustard seeds
1 chilli

Sterilise the jars. Put the vinegar and sugar in a pan and boil for 15–20 minutes. Add roughly chopped apricots and, if desired, the root ginger, peeled and cut in small pieces. Put spices and chilli in muslin bag and add to pan. Boil, uncovered, for 20 minutes. Remove spice bag. Pack in warmed jars. Seal while hot. Keep for at least 3 weeks before using.

TO CHOP ONIONS, CUT THE SKINNED ONION IN HALF, THEN PLACE THE FLAT SIDE DOWN ON A BOARD AND HOLD THE STALK END WHILE SLICING ACROSS

BANANA CHUTNEY

Makes 2 × 350 ml jars

3 bananas
2 onions
¾ cup malt vinegar
½ cup stoned and chopped dates
1 cup water
½ cup raisins
½ cup crystallised ginger, sliced
¼ cup sugar
½ teaspoon curry powder
½ teaspoon salt

First sterilise the jars. Mash bananas. Peel and chop onions. Put the bananas, onions, vinegar and dates in pan. Simmer for 20 minutes, stirring occasionally. Add rest of ingredients. Cook gently, uncovered, for about 1½ hours, or until thick. Pack, cover, cool and seal.

BEETROOT CHUTNEY

Makes 3 × 350 ml jars

1.5 kg beetroot
750 g onions
3½ cups sugar
1½ tablespoons salt
3½ cups vinegar
1½ teaspoons ground allspice
4 tablespoons plain flour
¼ cup extra vinegar

Sterilise the jars. Peel and mince beetroot and onions. Put in a pan with the sugar, salt, 3½ cups of vinegar and allspice. Boil for 30 minutes. Mix the flour and ¼ cup of vinegar together and stir into the boiling mixture. Boil 3–4 minutes longer, stirring occasionally. Pack in hot jars, cover until cool and seal.

BEETROOT AND TOMATO CHUTNEY

Makes 9 × 350 ml jars

1.75 kg beetroot
1.25 kg tomatoes
1.25 kg onions
5 cups vinegar
2¼ cups sugar
3 teaspoons turmeric
½ teaspoon cayenne pepper
4 teaspoons salt
2 tablespoons plain flour
¼ cup extra vinegar

Sterilise the jars. Gently simmer the beetroot in their skins until they become tender. Allow to cool a little. Peel and mince the cooked beetroot. Chop up the unskinned tomatoes and peeled onions, and cook them together with a minimum of water to prevent sticking, until they are tender. In another pan mix this tomato mixture with the cooked beetroot, 5 cups of vinegar, sugar, turmeric, cayenne pepper and salt. Bring to the boil, and continue boiling briskly for 20 minutes. Blend the flour into a paste with the extra vinegar. Add this to the pan. Stir steadily while boiling for 5 minutes. Pack in hot jars, cover until cool, then seal.

BLACKBERRY AND APPLE CHUTNEY

Makes 3 × 250 ml jars

1 kg blackberries
1 kg cooking apples
2 large onions
1 teaspoon salt
2 tablespoons peeled and grated root
  ginger
2 cloves garlic, chopped
100 g dried apricots
225 g raw sugar
1¼ cups tarragon vinegar

Sterilise the jars. Wash and drain blackberries. Peel, core and slice apples. Chop onions and put in pan with blackberries, apples, salt, ginger and garlic. Chop apricots. Add to pan with the sugar and vinegar. Stir well. Bring to boil. Cover. Reduce heat and simmer for about 1 hour, stirring occasionally to prevent sticking. Remove lid and boil a little more if still too moist. Pack and seal immediately.

HOT CHILLI CHUTNEY

Makes 2 × 350 ml jars

450 g chillies
1 onion, finely chopped
6 cloves garlic, crushed
4 tablespoons ground cumin
2 tablespoons turmeric
25 g root ginger, peeled and grated
1 tablespoon salt
1¼ cups oil
3 tablespoons sugar
1¼ cups vinegar

Sterilise the jars. Finely chop chillies, including seeds. Mix together the chillies, chopped onion, garlic, cumin, turmeric, ginger, salt and oil. Transfer to a heavy based pan and fry for 15 minutes, stirring often to prevent sticking. Add sugar and vinegar and bring to boil. Cover pan and boil for 10 minutes, stirring occasionally. Pack, cover until cool, then seal.

HOT CHOKO CHUTNEY

Makes 4 × 350 ml jars

3 large chokos
2 cooking apples
1 onion
225 g stoned dates
¼ cup crystallised ginger
2 cups malt vinegar
1 cup sugar
2 cups raisins
1 tablespoon salt
pinch of cayenne pepper

Peel and finely chop chokos, apples and onion. Finely chop dates and ginger. Mix all the ingredients in a non-metallic bowl and let stand overnight. Next day sterilise the jars. Put the ingredients from the bowl in pan. Boil for 20 minutes, or until tender. Pack, cover until cool and seal.

CUCUMBER CHUTNEY

Makes 6 × 350 ml jars

1.25 kg cucumbers
750 g onions
½ teaspoon peppercorns
4½ cups brown sugar
2¼ cups vinegar
2 cups sultanas
1 teaspoon ground ginger
½ teaspoon ground allspice
3 teaspoons salt
½ teaspoon cayenne pepper

Sterilise the jars. Peel and slice cucumbers and onions. Tie peppercorns in muslin bag. Put muslin bag and all ingredients in a pan. Bring to boil, stirring all the time, then reduce heat and simmer, uncovered, until thick. Stir frequently. Pack in jars, cover until cool, then seal.

CURRIED CUCUMBER CHUTNEY

Makes 6 × 350 ml jars

---

6 medium-sized cucumbers
3 onions
3 green or red peppers
½ cup salt
3¼ cups white vinegar
2 cups sugar
1 teaspoon celery seeds
1 teaspoon mustard seeds
2 teaspoons curry powder

Wash cucumbers and cut into 5-mm slices. Peel and slice onions. Chop peppers. Put all vegetables in a plastic bowl. Sprinkle with salt and cover with water. Leave for 2 hours. Sterilise the jars. Put the vinegar, sugar, celery and mustard seeds and curry powder into a pan. Stir over low heat until the sugar is dissolved, then bring to boil. Add drained vegetables. Simmer until chutney thickens – about 1½ hours. Pack in hot jars, cover until cool, then seal.

CUCUMBER AND CHERRY CHUTNEY

Makes 5 × 350 ml jars

---

750 g cucumbers
3 onions
500 g cherries
2 cups wine vinegar
1 cup sugar
1 tablespoon salt
1 teaspoon cumin seeds
1 teaspoon ground ginger
2 tablespoons arrowroot
4 tablespoons cold water

Sterilise the jars. Deseed and finely slice cucumbers. Finely slice the onions. Halve and stone cherries. Put all ingredients except arrowroot and water in pan and stir to dissolve sugar over low heat. Slowly bring to boil and simmer for 30 minutes. Blend the arrowroot and water, add to the pan and simmer for a further 5 minutes. Pack in hot jars, cover until cool and seal.

DAMSON CHUTNEY

Makes 5 × 350 ml jars

---

900 g stoned damsons
1 large onion, chopped
1 large apple, peeled and chopped
1 clove garlic, crushed
½ cup raisins
1½ cups malt vinegar
2 teaspoons whole pickling spices
1¼ cups sugar

Sterilise the jars. Put the fruit, vegetables, and half the vinegar in a pan. Tie the spices in a muslin bag and add to pan. Simmer steadily until fruit and vegetables become soft. Gradually add the remainder of the vinegar. Remove the muslin bag and stir in sugar until dissolved. Cook until thick. Pack in hot jars, cover, and seal when cool.

DATE CHUTNEY

Makes 2 × 350 ml jars

---

1 cooking apple
1 onion, chopped
1 cup vinegar
2 cloves
2 whole allspice
3-cm piece cinnamon stick
1 cup stoned dates

Sterilise the jars. Peel and chop apple. Put apple, onion and vinegar in pan and cook for 15 minutes, uncovered. Tie cloves, allspice and cinnamon stick in muslin bag. Add to pan with dates. Cook slowly for about 2 hours, stirring frequently. Remove the muslin bag of spices. Pack in hot jars, cover, and seal when cool.

DATE AND GINGER CHUTNEY

Makes 2 × 350 ml jars

---

375 g stoned dates
60 g preserved ginger
1 cup white vinegar
1 cup water
½ cup brown sugar
1 teaspoon chilli powder
1 teaspoon ground cinnamon

Sterilise the jars. Finely chop dates and ginger. In a pan put the vinegar, water and sugar. Stir over low heat until sugar dissolves. Increase heat and bring to boil. Add the chilli powder, cinnamon, ginger and dates. Bring back to boil, then reduce the heat and simmer for 10 minutes, until thick. Pour into hot jars, cover, and seal when cool. Refrigerate to store.

DO NOT USE COPPER, IRON OR BRASS PANS WHEN MAKING CHUTNEYS, RELISHES, PICKLES AND SAUCES

HOT EGGPLANT CHUTNEY

Makes 4 × 350 ml jars

1 kg eggplant, sliced
salt
1²/₃ cups white vinegar
½ cup raisins
1 cup brown sugar
1 tablespoon tomato paste
250 g onions, finely chopped
2 dried red chillies, chopped
4 sticks celery, chopped
5 cloves garlic, crushed

Put eggplant in a colander. Sprinkle with salt and let stand for 4 hours, then rinse and dry. Put vinegar, raisins, sugar and tomato paste in a bowl and stand for 4 hours. When ready to continue, sterilise the jars, then put all ingredients in a pan. Heat gently, stirring until sugar dissolves, then simmer until thick. Pack, cover, and seal when cool.

CHINESE-STYLE MIXED FRUIT CHUTNEY

Makes 4 × 350 ml jars

1 large pineapple
1 kg plums
1 kg apricots
1 kg soft brown sugar
1¼ cups white wine vinegar

Sterilise the jars. Peel pineapple and discard core. Skin and halve plums and apricots. Remove stones.

Cut all the fruit into small pieces and put in a pan with sugar and vinegar. Heat gently, stirring until the sugar dissolves. Simmer (adding more vinegar if necessary) until the fruit is soft. Pack at once. Cover until cool, then seal.

ELDERBERRY CHUTNEY

Makes 5 × 350 ml jars

1 kg elderberries
250 g onions, chopped
1¼ cups vinegar
125 g raisins, chopped
1 teaspoon ground ginger
1 teaspoon salt
½ teaspoon cayenne pepper
½ teaspoon mustard powder
1 teaspoon whole pickling spices
250 g sugar

First sterilise the jars. Strip elderberries from stalks. In a large pan simmer onion in the vinegar until soft. Add elderberries, raisins, ginger, salt, cayenne and mustard. Put pickling spices in muslin bag and add to pan. Simmer until mixture is soft. Stir in sugar until dissolved. Boil for 1½ hours, adding more vinegar if the mixture is too thick. Pack, cover, and seal when cool.

DON'T USE METALLIC TOPS FOR SEALING ANY PRESERVE CONTAINING VINEGAR

TANGY FRUIT CHUTNEY

Makes 4 × 350 ml jars

---

575 g cooking apples
450 g onions, chopped
100 g stoned and chopped dates
175 g raisins, chopped
juice and rind of 1 orange
225 g soft brown sugar
½ teaspoon turmeric
1¼ cups vinegar

Sterilise the jars. Peel, core and slice apples. Put in pan with onion, dates, raisins, strips of orange rind and juice. Add sugar, turmeric and vinegar and on low heat stir to dissolve sugar. Bring to boil, stirring frequently. Reduce heat, cover and let simmer for 1 hour. Remove lid and let cook for a further 15 minutes until thick. Pack, cover, and seal when cool.

HERB CHUTNEY

Makes 4 × 350 ml jars

1.5 kg cooking apples
1 kg onions
225 g raisins
225 g dried apricots
1⅔ cups white vinegar
2 tablespoons peeled and grated root ginger
350 g sugar
100 g chopped fresh mint or 50 g freshly chopped mixed herbs (leaves only)

Sterilise the jars. Peel, core and slice apples. Finely chop onions.

Roughly chop raisins and apricots. Mix fruit and onion together in pan. Add vinegar, ginger and sugar. Bring mixture to boil. Cover and reduce heat. Simmer over low heat until thickened. Near the end of the cooking time add the chopped herbs. Stir well and again bring to the boil quickly. Pack into hot jars, cover, and seal when cool.

KIWIFRUIT CHUTNEY

Makes 2 × 350 ml jars

---

2 onions
1 clove garlic, crushed
1 tablespoon chopped crystallised ginger
pinch of cayenne pepper
¾ cup brown sugar
¾ teaspoon ground cinnamon
¼ teaspoon ground cloves
¼ teaspoon ground allspice
½ cup raisins
¾ cup vinegar
500 g kiwifruit
2 cooking pears

Sterilise the jars. Peel and finely chop onions. Put onion, garlic, ginger, cayenne pepper, sugar, cinnamon, cloves, allspice, raisins and vinegar in pan. Bring to boil, stirring to dissolve sugar. Simmer for about 30 minutes. Peel kiwifruit and chop roughly. Peel, core and chop pears. Add kiwifruit and pears to pan, and simmer for 20 minutes, until mixture is thick, stirring occasionally. Pack, cover, and seal when cool.

MANGO CHUTNEY

Makes 4 × 350 ml jars

1 kg tomatoes
2 medium-sized onions, chopped
1 large cooking apple
1½ cups sugar
1 tablespoon salt
¼ teaspoon cayenne pepper
¼ teaspoon chilli powder
1 teaspoon ground cloves
2 cups white vinegar
1 × 560 g can mango slices
1 × 450 g can papaw pieces
2 teaspoons mustard seeds
1 cup water
1 cup sultanas
60 g preserved ginger

Sterilise the jars. Skin tomatoes and chop roughly. Put in pan and bring to boil. Reduce heat and cover, simmering until soft and pulpy. Remove from heat. Put through a fine sieve and return to pan. Add onion, cored and chopped apple, sugar and salt. Over a low heat stir until the sugar dissolves. Mix the cayenne, chilli powder and cloves with a little of the vinegar. Add to tomato mix with the drained and chopped mango and papaw, remaining vinegar, the mustard seeds and water. Bring to boil, then reduce heat to simmer for 30 minutes. Add sultanas and chopped ginger. Simmer until mixture has thickened. Pack, cover, and seal when cool.

MARROW CHUTNEY

Makes 8 × 350 ml jars

2 kg peeled and deseeded marrow
salt
a small piece peeled root ginger
6 chillies
6 cloves
5 cups vinegar
500 g sugar
250 g raisins
250 g onions, chopped
2 tablespoons mustard powder
2 tablespoons turmeric

Cut the marrow into small cubes. Put in a non-metallic bowl and sprinkle with salt. Let stand overnight. Next day sterilise the jars, then put root ginger, chillies and cloves in a muslin bag. Put in a pan with the vinegar, sugar, raisins and chopped onion. Simmer for 15 minutes. Add the drained marrow, the mustard and the turmeric. Cook until the marrow is tender. Remove the muslin bag. Pack, cover, and seal when cool.

TO CHOP ONIONS, CUT THE SKINNED ONION IN HALF, THEN PLACE THE FLAT SIDE DOWN ON A BOARD AND HOLD THE STALK END WHILE SLICING ACROSS

MIXED MINTED CHUTNEY

Makes 4 × 350 ml jars

---

3 green peppers
3 cooking apples
3 large tomatoes
4 onions
3 cups vinegar
1¾ cups brown sugar
2 teaspoons mustard powder
2 teaspoons salt
½ cup chopped fresh mint
250 g raisins

Sterilise the jars. Deseed peppers and finely chop flesh. Peel, core and chop apples. Peel and chop tomatoes and onions. Put the vinegar, sugar, mustard and salt in a large pan. Bring to boil. Add the tomatoes, apples, peppers, onions and chopped mint. Simmer for 30 minutes. Add raisins. Simmer a further 30 minutes. Remove from heat. Pack, cover, and seal when cool.

HOT INDIAN PATNA CHUTNEY

Makes 4 × 350 ml jars

---

1 kg cooking apples
9 cups malt vinegar
500 g onions, chopped
8 cloves garlic, crushed
1 kg dark brown sugar
50 g salt
4 teaspoons cayenne pepper
500 g raisins, chopped
125 g mustard powder
150 g ground ginger

Peel, core and slice apples. Put vinegar, apples, onions, garlic, sugar and salt in a large pan and simmer until soft. Rub through a sieve and put in a non-metallic bowl. Stir in the cayenne pepper, chopped raisins, mustard and ginger. Cover and allow to stand overnight. Next day sterilise the jars, stir mixture well, pack in jars and seal.

PAPAW CHUTNEY

Makes 2 × 350 ml jars

---

500 g papaws, deseeded
¼ cup stoned dates
2 teaspoons whole pickling spices
1½ cups malt vinegar
1 onion, chopped
¼ cup sultanas
2 teaspoons salt
1¼ cups brown sugar
2 teaspoons cornflour
a little cold water

Sterilise the jars. Chop papaws and dates into small pieces. Tie the pickling spices in a muslin bag. Put muslin bag, vinegar, papaws, dates, onion, sultanas, salt and sugar in a pan. Bring to boil. Simmer for 1½ hours, stirring occasionally. Blend cornflour and water to a smooth paste. Add to the mixture. Boil for 5 minutes, stirring continuously. Pack into hot jars and seal.

DO NOT USE COPPER, IRON OR BRASS PANS WHEN MAKING CHUTNEYS, RELISHES, PICKLES AND SAUCES

PEACH CHUTNEY

Makes 3 × 350 ml jars

---

12 peaches
450 g onions, chopped
2 tablespoons peeled and grated root
   ginger
2 cloves garlic, crushed
100 g stoned dates
225 g raw sugar
1¼ cups vinegar
pepper
salt
juice of 1 orange
dash of red wine

Sterilise the jars. Blanch peaches with boiling water, let stand for 1 minute then peel and stone. Cut into thick slices. Put onions in a pan with peaches, ginger and garlic. Chop dates. Add to the pan with the sugar and vinegar. Add a generous sprinkling of pepper and salt. Stir well. Bring to the boil, stirring continuously until the sugar has dissolved. Cover the pan. Reduce heat and simmer for about 45 minutes, until mixture thickens. Add orange juice and wine. Stir frequently during cooking to prevent sticking to the pan. Pack into hot jars, cover until cool and seal.

PEAR AND GOOSEBERRY CHUTNEY

Makes 3 × 350 ml jars

1 kg cooking pears
1 kg gooseberries
2 large onions
25 g root ginger
50 g sultanas
175 g sugar
1¼ cups cider vinegar
1 teaspoon turmeric
2 teaspoons salt

Sterilise the jars. Peel, core and chop pears. Top and tail gooseberries. Peel and finely chop onion and ginger. Put all the ingredients in pan. Stir well. Bring to boil, then reduce heat and simmer for 1 hour, until fruit is pulpy and chutney is thickened. Pack in hot jars. Cover until cool, then seal.

PLUM CHUTNEY

Makes 4 × 350 ml jars

2.25 kg plums
350 g cooking apples
450 g onions
2 tablespoons peeled and grated root ginger
1 tablespoon mustard powder
1 teaspoon salt
a little pepper
450 g sugar
1 cup vinegar

Sterilise the jars. Stone, halve and roughly chop plums. Peel, core and chop apples. Chop onions. Put plums, apples and onions in pan. Add ginger, mustard and salt. Season with pepper. Add sugar and vinegar. Bring to boil, then lower heat and simmer for about 2 hours, stirring frequently. Pack in hot jars. Cover until cool, then seal.

PLUM AND PEAR CHUTNEY

Makes 4 × 350 ml jars

---

1 kg cooking plums
1 kg cooking pears
450 g onions, chopped
1¼ cups tarragon vinegar
225 g stoned dates
2 tablespoons peeled and grated root
   ginger
225 g soft brown sugar
2 cloves garlic, crushed

Sterilise the jars. Stone and halve plums. Peel, core and slice pears and add to pan. Add plums, onion, vinegar, chopped dates, ginger, sugar and garlic. Stir well. Bring to boil. Cover pan, reduce heat and simmer for about 1½ hours. Stir occasionally. Pack in hot jars. Cover until cool, then seal.

PRUNE AND CHOKO CHUTNEY

Makes 4 × 350 ml jars

---

3 large chokos
2 cooking apples
1 onion
¼ cup crystallised ginger
2 cups stoned prunes
1 cup raisins
1 cup sugar
2 cups malt vinegar

Peel and finely chop chokos, apple and onion. Finely chop ginger,

prunes and raisins. Mix all ingredients together in a non-metallic bowl and leave overnight. Next day sterilise the jars, then transfer contents of bowl to a pan and bring to boil. Boil for 20 minutes until all is tender. Pack in hot jars, cover, and seal when cool.

PUMPKIN CHUTNEY

Makes 4 × 350 ml jars

---

500 g tomatoes
1.25 kg peeled and deseeded pumpkin
750 g soft brown sugar
250 g onions, sliced
125 g sultanas
2⅓ cups tarragon vinegar
2 cloves garlic, crushed
2½ teaspoons ground ginger
2 teaspoons ground black pepper
2 teaspoons ground allspice
2½ tablespoons salt

Sterilise the jars. Peel and slice the tomatoes. Cut pumpkin into small pieces, and put in pan with all other ingredients. Stir over low heat until the sugar has dissolved. Bring to the boil, then simmer gently until soft. Pack into hot jars, cover until cool and seal.

STORE YOUR PRESERVES IN A COOL, AIRY, DRY, DARK PLACE

QUINCE CHUTNEY

Makes 4 × 350 ml jars

---

3 large quinces
2 large cooking apples
2 large onions
3 cups malt vinegar
1½ cups brown sugar
2½ teaspoons salt
½ teaspoon ground ginger
½ teaspoon mustard powder
½ teaspoon curry powder

Sterilise the jars. Wash, peel, core and mince or finely process the quinces, apples and onions. Put in a large pan and add all other ingredients. Boil the mixture for 2 hours. Stir frequently to make sure that the mixture does not stick to the pan, especially towards the end of the cooking time. Pack into hot jars, cover until cool and seal.

RHUBARB AND APPLE CHUTNEY

Makes 3 × 350 ml jars

---

450 g cooking apples
450 g trimmed rhubarb
225 g onions, chopped
225 g dried figs
350 g soft brown sugar
1 teaspoon ground ginger
1 teaspoon ground mixed spice
1¾ cups vinegar

Sterilise the jars. Peel, core and slice apples and put in pan with sliced rhubarb, chopped onion, chopped figs, sugar, spices and vinegar. Stir well and bring to boil. Cover pan and reduce heat. Simmer for 1 hour. Uncover pan and simmer for about another 30 minutes, stirring occasionally. Pack in hot jars, cover, and seal when cool.

RHUBARB AND GINGER CHUTNEY

Makes 6 × 350 ml jars

---

375 g peeled and cored apples
375 g onions
30 g peeled root ginger
2 cloves garlic
1.5 kg rhubarb, sliced
2 cups wine vinegar
1 tablespoon tomato paste
3 teaspoons salt
2 teaspoons paprika
juice of 1 orange
3 cups sugar

Sterilise the jars. Mince or process apples, onions, ginger and garlic and put in a pan with all the other ingredients except the sugar. Stir together well. Simmer until ingredients are pulpy. When the mixture has thickened, add the sugar, stirring until it has all dissoved. Bring back to the boil and boil rapidly until the chutney has thickened. Pack into hot jars. Cover until cool, then seal.

TAMARILLO CHUTNEY

Makes 6 × 350 ml jars

24 tamarillos
4 cooking apples
4 onions
½ cup crystallised ginger
1½ cups stoned dates
5 cups brown sugar
2 cups malt vinegar
1½ cups raisins
1 × 454 g can pineapple pieces
2 teaspoons ground mixed spice
1 teaspoon cayenne pepper
1 tablespoon salt

Sterilise the jars. Blanch tamarillos in boiling water for 30 seconds. Drain and remove skins. Cut or slice roughly. Peel and core the apples. Finely chop up the apples, onions, ginger and the dates. Put all the ingredients together in a large pan and bring slowly to the boil. Reduce heat and simmer for 1½–2 hours, until mixture thickens. Stir occasionally to prevent catching. Pack in hot jars. Cover until cool, then seal.

DON'T FORGET TO LABEL AND
DATE YOUR PRESERVES

AVOID USING JARS THAT ARE
NOT PERFECT. THEY MAY BREAK
WHEN A HOT PRESERVE IS
POURED INTO THEM

GREEN TOMATO CHUTNEY

Makes 4 × 350 ml jars

1.5 kg green tomatoes
2 cooking apples
1 large onion
2 tablespoons salt
1 cup stoned prunes
1 teaspoon peppercorns
1 tablespoon mustard seeds
2 cloves garlic, bruised
2 cups brown sugar
2 cups vinegar

Wash tomatoes. Wash, peel and core apples. Mince or finely process tomatoes, apples and onion. Put in a non-metallic bowl and mix in the salt. Let stand overnight. Cover prunes with water and let stand overnight also. Next day sterilise the jars, then drain fruit and onion mix and prunes. Finely chop prunes. Put fruit and onion and prunes in a pan. Tie peppercorns, mustard seeds and garlic in a muslin bag. Add muslin bag and rest of ingredients to pan. Bring to the boil, stirring to dissolve sugar. Reduce heat, then simmer gently, stirring occasionally until thick. Remove muslin bag. Pack, cover until cool and seal.

RED TOMATO CHUTNEY

Makes 4 × 350 ml jars

---

1 kg ripe tomatoes
450 g onions
225 g sultanas
175 g raw sugar
²⁄₃ cup vinegar
2 cloves garlic, crushed
1½ teaspoons coriander seeds
1½ teaspoons ground ginger

Sterilise the jars. Stand tomatoes in boiling water for 30 seconds, then drain, peel and chop. Peel and finely chop the onions. Chop the sultanas. Mix all the ingredients together in a pan. Bring to the boil, stirring continuously to prevent catching. Cover pan, reduce heat and simmer for 1¼ hours, stirring occasionally. Then remove lid and continue cooking for a further 15 minutes. Pack into hot jars, cover, and seal when cool. Allow to mature for 1 month before using.

TOMATO AND RED PEPPER CHUTNEY

Makes 3 × 350 ml jars

---

4 large red peppers
4 medium-sized onions
500 g tomatoes
2 tablespoons salt
1½ cups sugar
2 cups white vinegar
1 tablespoon mustard seeds
2 tablespoons plain flour
¼ teaspoon turmeric
¼ teaspoon paprika
½ cup water

Deseed peppers and finely chop. Peel onions and tomatoes and finely chop. Put peppers, onion and tomato in a bowl and sprinkle with salt. Let stand for a few hours. When ready to continue cooking, sterilise the jars, then drain peppers, onion and tomato and put in a large pan. Add the sugar, vinegar and mustard seeds. Stir well over low heat until the sugar has dissolved. Bring to the boil and boil steadily for 10 minutes. Blend flour, turmeric, paprika and water into a smooth paste. Stir into mixture until boiling again, then reduce heat. Simmer for a further 10 minutes. Pack into hot jars, cover until cool and seal.

UNCOOKED CHUTNEY

Makes 6 × 350 ml jars

---

750 g cooking apples
500 g raisins
250 g onions, chopped
750 g soft brown sugar
1¼ cups malt vinegar
1 tablespoon salt
2 teaspoons ground pickling spice

Peel and core apples. Put through a mincer with the raisins and the onions, or process. Place in a non-metallic bowl with all other ingredients. Cover and let stand, stirring occasionally until the sugar has dissolved. Sterilise jars, pack chutney into them and seal.

ZUCCHINI CHUTNEY

Makes 4 × 350 ml jars

---

750 g zucchini, sliced
1 tablespoon salt
250 g ripe tomatoes
125 g onions, chopped
2 cups sugar
1½ cups tarragon vinegar
¼ cup sultanas
1 teaspoon ground cinnamon
coarsely grated rind of 1 orange
½ cup chopped walnuts

Put zucchini in colander. Sprinkle with salt and leave for 2 hours. Rinse and dry. Sterilise the jars. Put the zucchini in a pan with all the remaining ingredients except the walnuts. Heat gently, stirring until the sugar dissolves. Simmer until the mixture thickens, then stir in the walnuts. Pack into hot jars, cover until cool and seal.

$\mathcal{R}$ELISHES

Relish usually refers to a condiment produced from vegetables and fruits, flavoured and spiced and cooked in vinegar, which acts as a preservative. Relish can be sweet or sour, spiced or plain. Generally, 'chutney' is a sweetened mixture that is thick and of an even texture, with a mellow taste, whereas 'relish' is a mixture of similar ingredients that are chopped more finely and cooked for less time, so retaining the texture of the ingredients. The produce should be ripe, but not over-ripe, and should be discarded if diseased. Fruits and vegetables should be washed, peeled, and seeded or stoned, according to type. They may be coarsely minced, chopped, or sliced. Sugar, flavourings and vinegar are added and everything cooked until soft. Use either white or brown malt vinegar, of good quality, as cheaper vinegars do not contain sufficient acetic acid to act as a preservative. Don't use iron, brass or copper pans for cooking.

The cooked fruit determines the colour of the product. Brown sugar and golden syrup (unless the recipe states otherwise) will vary the flavour and darken the colour. If the product is tasted while still warm, a false idea of flavour will be given. It may sometimes seem to be too spicy or hot, but this will modify with storage.

The jars, bottles, lids and corks used to pack the product should always be thoroughly washed and sterilised. Metal lids should be avoided on any product containing vinegar, which corrodes the metal. Relishes should be packed while hot and stored for at least 6 to 8 weeks to enable the flavour to develop and mature. They should be stored in a dark, dry, cool place; warm or damp storage areas induce the growth of mould.

APPLE AND MINT RELISH

Makes 3 × 350 ml jars

1.5 kg cooking apples
4 cups vinegar
100 g whole pickling spices
2 dried red chillies
½ teaspoon coriander seeds
1 teaspoon black peppercorns
3 cups brown sugar
2 teaspoons salt
2 tablespoons chopped fresh mint

Sterilise the jars. Put the apples in a pan with the vinegar. Bring slowly to boiling point. Tie the pickling spices, chillies, coriander and peppercorns in a muslin bag. Add to the pan with the sugar and salt, stirring until the sugar has dissolved. Simmer until thickened. Remove bag. Stir in mint. Pack in hot jars, cover until cool and seal.

BEETROOT AND APPLE RELISH

Makes 4 × 350 ml jars

---

10 beetroot
2 large cooking apples
2 large onions
1½ cups water
2 cups white vinegar
1 cup sugar
5-cm piece cinnamon stick
3 teaspoons ground ginger
½ cup plain flour

Sterilise the jars. Peel beetroot. Cut off stems. Chop into 1-cm cubes. Peel and core the apples.

Chop into 1-cm cubes. Peel onions and chop up roughly. Put 1 cup of the water, vinegar and sugar into a pan. Stir over medium heat until the sugar dissolves. Bring to boil, then add the beetroot, apples, onion and cinnamon. Bring back to the boil, then reduce heat and simmer, covered, for 40 minutes. Remove cinnamon stick. Blend ginger and flour to a paste with remaining ½ cup of water. Gradually stir into the mixture and heat until boiling. Reduce heat and simmer uncovered for 45 minutes, stirring occasionally. Pack into hot jars, cover until cool and seal.

BEETROOT RELISH

Makes 3 × 350 ml jars

---

450 g beetroot
450 g cooking apples
350 g onions
255 g dark brown sugar
1¾ cups vinegar
2 large cloves garlic
1 teaspoon paprika
1 teaspoon turmeric
1 tablespoon peeled and finely
*   chopped root ginger*
1 cinnamon stick

Sterilise the jars. Peel the beetroot. Peel and core the apples. Grate both into a pan. Finely chop the onions. Add to the pan with all the other ingredients. Bring the mixture to the boil and cover the pan. Reduce heat and simmer for about 1½ hours. Stir occasionally. Remove cinnamon. Pack into hot jars, cover until cool and seal.

BEETROOT AND RAISIN RELISH

Makes 3 × 350 ml jars

1 kg beetroot
500 g onions
500 g raisins
1 tablespoon salt
6 whole allspice
6 peppercorns
1-cm piece peeled root ginger
6 cloves
1½ cups white vinegar
1¾ cups sugar

Sterilise the jars. Wash beetroot. Trim roots and stalks and cook in boiling, salted water until tender. Drain. Slip off the skin and cut flesh into small cubes. Peel and chop onions. Put beetroot, onion, raisins and salt in pan. Tie the allspice, peppercorns, ginger and cloves in a muslin bag. Add to the pan with the vinegar and sugar. Bring to the boil. Simmer until it thickens. Remove bag of spices. Pack in hot jars, cover until cool and seal.

CHILLI RELISH

Makes 3 × 350 ml jars

500 g tomatoes
4 onions
2 red peppers
3 red chillies
2 cucumbers
3 tablespoons salt
2 cups white vinegar
¾ cup white sugar
¾ cup brown sugar
1 tablespoon mustard seeds
2 tablespoons plain flour
2 teaspoons paprika
½ teaspoon chilli powder
½ cup water

Peel the tomatoes. Peel onions. Seed peppers and chillies. Peel and seed cucumbers. Chop them all finely and put in a non-metallic bowl. Sprinkle with salt. Stand for 3 hours, then drain and rinse. Sterilise the jars. Put the vinegar, sugars and mustard seeds in a large pan. Stir over low heat until sugar dissolves. Increase heat and bring to boil. Add fruit and vegetables, bring back to boil, reduce heat and simmer, uncovered, for 5 minutes. Blend flour, paprika, chilli powder and water to a smooth paste. Add to the fruit and vegetable mixture and stir constantly until the mixture boils and thickens. Reduce heat and simmer for 25 minutes. Pack in jars, cover until cool and seal.

CORN AND PEPPER RELISH

Makes 4 × 350 ml jars

---

4 green peppers
500 g onions
4 cups sweetcorn kernels
3 cups white vinegar
1 tablespoon salt
2 cups sugar
3 tablespoons plain flour
1 teaspoon turmeric
2 teaspoons mustard powder

Sterilise the jars. Deseed and chop peppers. Peel and chop onions. Put corn, peppers and onion in pan. Add vinegar, salt and sugar. Bring to the boil and simmer, uncovered, for 1 hour. Mix flour, turmeric and mustard in a bowl with ¼ cup of the hot vinegar from pan. Blend to a smooth paste. Stir into vegetable mixture and boil for 5 minutes. Pack, cover until cool and seal.

CUCUMBER AND RED PEPPER RELISH

Makes 2 × 350 ml jars

---

750 g cucumbers
2 teaspoons salt
2 large red peppers
1 tablespoon lime juice
¾ cup wine vinegar
2 teaspoons mustard seeds

Cut cucumbers lengthways. Remove seeds. Mince or process flesh coarse-ly, then put in sieve. Sprinkle with salt and stand for 1 hour. Sterilise the jars. Deseed peppers and thinly slice. Mix peppers and lime juice in a bowl. Squeeze excess moisture from cucumber. In a large pan bring the vinegar to the boil and add cucumber, peppers and lime juice, and mustard seeds. Simmer for 10 minutes. Pack in hot jars, cover until cool and seal.

CURRY RELISH

Makes 4 × 350 ml jars

---

250 g eggplant
250 g carrots
175 g onions
250 g tiny cauliflower florets
125 g peas
125 g sweetcorn kernels
1 tablespoon salt
1 tablespoon whole pickling spices
2 cups cider vinegar
1 cup brown sugar
1½ teaspoons curry powder
1 teaspoon coriander seeds
½ teaspoon ground ginger
⅔ cup water
¼ cup flaked almonds
1 tablespoon cornflour
2 tablespoons extra water

Halve eggplant lengthways. Slice across very thinly and put in bowl. Grate carrot and onion into bowl, add the remaining vegetables and the salt. Just cover with water. Let stand overnight. Next day, sterilise the jars, then drain vegetables well, squeezing out as much water as possible. Tie pickling spices in muslin bag and put in large pan with vinegar, sugar, spices and the ⅔ cup of water. Bring to boil and simmer for 20 minutes. Add vegetables and almonds. Cover and simmer for 10 minutes. Remove lid. Boil fast for 7 minutes, then remove the muslin bag. Blend cornflour and extra water into a paste. Add to pan. Boil for 3 minutes, stirring continuously. Pack in hot jars and seal.

INDIAN EGGPLANT RELISH

Makes 4 × 350 ml jars

2 eggplant
3 tablespoons salt
3 red peppers
500 g onions, quartered
3 tablespoons oil
2 red chillies, finely chopped
2 cloves garlic, crushed
2 tablespoons plain flour
1 cup white vinegar
½ cup water
⅓ cup sugar
1 teaspoon turmeric
1 tablespoon mustard seeds
1 teaspoon garam masala

First sterilise the jars. Cut eggplant into slices 2.5 cm thick. Cover with the salt and stand 30 minutes. Rinse and dry eggplant, then quarter each piece. Seed peppers, cut into 2.5-cm cubes, put into pan of boiling water and boil for 3 minutes. Remove from pan. Rinse. Put

onions and eggplant in the same boiling water, boil 3 minutes and drain. Heat oil in a large pan. Sauté chillies and garlic for 3 minutes. Add other vegetables. Sauté 1 minute. Mix flour and vinegar to a smooth paste, and add to saucepan with water, sugar, turmeric, mustard seeds and garam masala. Stir over medium heat until thickened. Add to pan. Stir until boiling. Simmer for 1 minute. Pack in hot jars, cover until cool and seal.

LEMON RELISH

Makes 2 × 250 ml jars

1 red pepper
2 large lemons
6 large spring onions
2 large sticks celery
1 fresh red chilli
4 sprigs parsley, chopped
½ cup tarragon vinegar
2 tablespoons sugar
1 teaspoon salt
½ teaspoon mustard powder
½ teaspoon ground cardamom

Sterilise the jars. Core and deseed pepper. Pare rind from lemon, discarding white pith. Coarsely mince the lemon rind and flesh, and all the vegetables. Put all ingredients into a pan. Bring to the boil, then reduce heat to simmer for 15 minutes. Pack into hot jars, cover to cool and seal.

MINT RELISH

Makes 4 × 350 ml jars

---

2 cups cider vinegar
250 g sugar
1 teaspoon mustard powder
1 teaspoon curry powder
500 g cucumber
a little salt
500 g ripe tomatoes
1 red or green pepper
250 g onions
1 cup raisins
½ cup chopped fresh mint

Sterilise the jars. In a small pan bring the vinegar to the boil. Add sugar, mustard and curry powders. Let cool. Peel and deseed cucumber. Cut into 1-cm dice and sprinkle with a little salt. Dice tomatoes. Seed and dice pepper. Finely chop onions. Cut raisins coarsely. Drain cucumber and put in bowl. Add other prepared fruit and vegetables, raisins and mint. Pour the vinegar mixture over the top and mix well. Pack, cover until cool and seal.

GREEN PEPPER RELISH

Makes 3 × 350 ml jars

---

1 kg green peppers
2 tablespoons salt
2½ cups vinegar
1½ cups sugar

Deseed peppers, chop finely and put in non-metallic bowl. Sprinkle with salt. Cover and stand for 12 hours. Next day, sterilise the jars, then drain peppers. Rinse with cold water and let stand in sieve to drain thoroughly. Put peppers, vinegar and sugar in a pan. Boil gently for 45 minutes, until mixture thickens and peppers become clear. Pack in hot jars, cover until cool and seal.

SWEET PEPPER RELISH

Makes 3 × 350 ml jars

---

2 green peppers
2 red peppers
1 onion
1 stick celery
1½ cups white vinegar
1 cup sugar
2 teaspoons salt
200 g cabbage
2 tablespoons arrowroot
¼ cup cold water

Sterilise the jars. Deseed the peppers. Finely chop the peppers, onion and celery. Place chopped vegetables in a large saucepan and cover with boiling water. Let stand for 5 minutes. Drain. Cover again with boiling water. Let stand for 10 minutes. Drain. Put vinegar, sugar and salt in a pan. Bring to boil. Simmer for 5 minutes. Chop cabbage finely and add to pan with rest of vegetables; boil for 3 minutes. Blend arrowroot and water to a smooth paste. Stir into vegetables until mixture boils. Boil for 3 minutes. Pack into hot jars, cover until cool and seal.

PINEAPPLE RELISH

Makes 2 × 350 ml jars

2 × 450 g cans pineapple pieces
2 fresh green chillies
2 fresh red chillies
250 g onions
1 blade mace
15 g peeled root ginger
1 tablespoon mustard powder
1⅓ cups vinegar
2 teaspoons salt

Sterilise the jars. Drain pineapple, reserving juice. Mince or process pineapple coarsely with the chillies and onions. Tie the mace and root ginger in a muslin bag. Blend mustard with 1¼ cups of the pineapple juice. Boil all ingredients together in pan until the onion is cooked and there is just sufficient liquid in pan to prevent sticking. Stir frequently. Pack into hot jars, cover until cool and seal.

PLUM RELISH

Makes 2 × 350 ml jars

500 g red plums
2 cooking pears
1 large orange
1 cup sugar
¾ cup wine vinegar
½ cup orange juice
2 teaspoons salt

Sterilise the jars. Stone and chop plums. Peel and dice pears. Cut orange rind into fine strips. Place in a pan with the plums, pears and sugar. Add vinegar, orange juice and salt to pan. Heat gently, stirring until sugar has dissolved. Simmer for 15 minutes until fruit is just tender. Pack into hot jars, cover until cool and seal.

SPICY PLUM RELISH

Makes 6 × 350 ml jars

2.25 kg plums
450 g onions
350 g cooking apples
1 teaspoon salt
1 tablespoon mustard powder
2 tablespoons peeled and grated root
    ginger
2 large cloves garlic
8 cloves
1 cinnamon stick
450 g sugar
1 cup vinegar
ground black pepper

Sterilise the jars. Halve plums, stone and chop roughly. Chop onions. Peel, core and roughly chop apples. Put plums, onion and apple in a large pan with salt, mustard, ginger and crushed garlic. Tie the cloves and broken cinnamon stick in a muslin bag. Add to pan. Add the sugar and vinegar. Season with generous sprinkling of black pepper. Bring to boil, stirring often. Reduce heat and cover the pan. Simmer for about 2½ hours, until the volume is reduced by half. Stir frequently to prevent sticking. If necessary, reduce heat slightly, to a very gentle simmer. Pack in hot jars and seal.

RED-CURRANT RELISH

Makes 2 × 350 ml jars

1 kg red currants
1 kg onions
225 g raw sugar
50 g root ginger, peeled and grated
4 cloves garlic, crushed
1 1/4 cups red wine vinegar
1 teaspoon turmeric
1 teaspoon ground cardamom
1 teaspoon salt

Sterilise the jars. Top and tail the red currants. Finely chop onions and put in pan with the red currants. Add all other ingredients and bring to the boil. Reduce heat and simmer, covered, for about 1 hour until fruit is soft and pulpy. Stir frequently. Pack in hot jars, cover until cool, then seal.

RHUBARB RELISH

Makes 5 × 350 ml jars

900 g rhubarb
1 teaspoon ground cinnamon
1/2 teaspoon ground mixed spice
1/4 teaspoon ground cloves
1/4 teaspoon ground nutmeg
900 g sugar
2/3 cup cider vinegar
2/3 cup water
225 g raisins

Sterilise the jars. Cut the rhubarb into 2.5-cm cubes. Put the spices in a pan with the sugar, vinegar and water. Bring to the boil and simmer for about 25 minutes. Add rhubarb and raisins. Return to the boil, and simmer for a further 40 minutes. Pack into hot jars, cover until cool and seal.

RUNNER BEAN RELISH

Makes 5 × 350 ml jars

1.8 kg runner beans
1/2 tablespoon turmeric
900 g sugar
4 cups cider vinegar
3 tablespoons cornflour
1 tablespoon celery salt
4 tablespoons mustard powder

Sterilise the jars. Top, tail and string beans. Cut in thin slices diagonally. Boil a pan of water, add turmeric, and cook beans until tender (but do not overcook). Put sugar and vinegar in another pan, and bring to the boil for 10 minutes. Stir until the sugar is dissolved. Mix together the cornflour, celery salt and mustard. Stir to a smooth paste with 2 tablespoons of the vinegar mixture. Add this paste to the boiling vinegar and stir until the syrup is thick and smooth. Add the beans. Pack in hot jars, cover until cool and seal.

SWEETCORN RELISH

Makes 4 × 350 ml jars

2 large onions
1 green pepper
1 red pepper
4 sticks celery
4 tablespoons corn oil
1 teaspoon salt
1 large clove garlic
2 carrots
675 g sweetcorn kernels
50 g sugar
1¾ cups vinegar

Sterilise the jars. Finely chop onions. Remove stalks, seeds and pith from peppers and chop finely. Chop celery. Heat oil. Add onions, peppers and celery and fry until soft but not brown. Add salt and crushed garlic. Cut carrots into small cubes. Add to pan with remaining ingredients. Bring to the boil and cook, uncovered, for 15 minutes, stirring occasionally. Pack into hot jars, cover until cool and seal.

TOMATO AND ONION RELISH

Makes 3 × 350 ml jars

1 kg ripe tomatoes
1 kg onions
4 large cloves garlic
175 g sugar
1¼ cups white vinegar
1 teaspoon paprika
½ teaspoon turmeric

Sterilise the jars. Put tomatoes in a large bowl. Cover with boiling water and let stand for about 30 seconds. Drain, peel tomatoes and finely chop them. Finely chop onions and mince garlic. Put in a pan with the tomatoes. Add all the other ingredients. Bring mixture to the boil. Reduce heat to a simmer and cook, uncovered, for 1 hour. Stir occasionally. Pack into hot jars, cover until cool and seal.

VINEGARS

Apart from malt vinegar and pickling vinegar, many other types of vinegar can be of use. When making flavoured vinegars it is best to use a wine vinegar, but white and cider vinegar may also be used. Herb, fruit and vegetable vinegars are excellent when added to salad dressings and sauces, or when used as a flavouring for fish. They can also be used for pickling onions, new potatoes, eggs and fruits, or in sauces, ketchups and relishes.

Fruit vinegars are a very good way of utilising over-ripe soft fruit. Raspberries are most often used, but any of the berry fruits will make a pleasant vinegar. Try blueberries. Discard the stalks and any leaves, and put the fruit in a non-metallic bowl. Using a wooden spoon, crush the fruit and pour the vinegar over the top. Allow 2 cups of vinegar for every 400 g of fruit. To get a nice clear, bright colour with fruit such as raspberries, use a white vinegar, but malt vinegar is quite suitable for blackberries and blackcurrants.

For herb vinegars, rosemary, sage, mint, thyme, lemon balm, basil, chives, marjoram and tarragon are all suitable for flavouring. If mixing herbs, balance the more delicately flavoured ones with those that are stronger. Use rosemary or thyme, which are so very markedly flavoured, in smaller quantities than lemon balm or marjoram. Whole spices are the best for making a spiced vinegar, as ground ones will make the vinegar cloudy. The spices used may be varied according to personal taste.

Flavoured vinegars store well, but the original flavouring may be overlaid after steeping. Fresh flavouring can be added. As with jams and jellies, sterilising of the jars, bottles, lids and corks, is a necessary adjunct to preparation. Bottle tops must be non-metallic.

BLACKBERRY VINEGAR

Makes 2 × 350 ml bottles

---

500 g blackberries or other berries
2⅓ cups white wine vinegar
sugar

Wash berries, drain and put in bowl. Crush with a wooden spoon and add vinegar. Cover. Stand for 4 days, stirring occasionally. Sterilise the bottles when ready to complete cooking. Strain vinegar through a jelly bag or double muslin, measure the liquid and return to pan. To each 2 cups of liquid add 750 g of sugar. Stir over a gentle heat until sugar dissolves, then boil rapidly for 10 minutes. Allow to cool. Bottle and seal.

BOYSENBERRY VINEGAR

Makes about 430 ml

---

4 cups boysenberries
1 cup malt vinegar
sugar

Wash berries, drain and put in a non-metallic bowl. Cover with vinegar and let stand for 24 hours. Sterilise the bottles. Mash the fruit. Strain off the juice, measure it and pour into a pan. To each 2½ cups of juice add 2 cups of sugar. Stir to dissolve sugar and boil for 20 minutes. Cool. Pour into bottles and cork. To make a refreshing drink add 2 tablespoons to 1 cup of water.

CELERY VINEGAR

Makes 2 × 350 ml bottles

---

250 g celery or 15 g celery seeds
2⅓ cups white wine vinegar
1 tablespoon salt

Sterilise the bottles. Clean and chop whole celery. Pack in prepared bottles. If celery seeds are used, divide them between the bottles. Boil the vinegar in a pan with the salt. Pour the hot vinegar onto the celery or seeds. Cover and leave until cold. Seal the bottles. Stand for 3 weeks, then strain and rebottle in sterilised bottles. Seal firmly.

CHILLI VINEGAR

Makes 1 × 200 ml bottle

---

5 small hot chillies
¾ cup white vinegar

Wash the chillies and place in small, sterilised bottle. Cover with vinegar. Seal. As vinegar readily absorbs the hot flavour of the chillies, it is ready for use in about 2 weeks. Remove the chillies then and use as required.

DON'T USE METALLIC TOPS FOR SEALING ANY PRESERVE CONTAINING VINEGAR

CRANBERRY VINEGAR

Makes 4 × 350 ml bottles

2 kg ripe cranberries
10 cups white wine vinegar
sugar

Put washed fruit in non-metallic bowl. Crush it and add vinegar. Cover with a cloth. Stand for 10 days, stirring daily. To complete process, sterilise bottles, then strain the vinegar through a jelly bag. Measure the liquid and add 200 g of sugar to each cup of liquid. Put in pan and stir over low heat to dissolve sugar, then boil for 10 minutes until the vinegar is syrupy. Bottle and seal.

CUCUMBER VINEGAR

Makes 2 × 300 ml bottles

5 small cucumbers
2 onions
2⅓ cups white wine vinegar

Peel and finely chop the cucumber and onion. Put into a non-metallic bowl with the vinegar. Cover and let stand for 10 days, stirring occasionally. To complete process, sterilise bottles and drain off the vinegar. Bottle it and seal.

GARLIC VINEGAR

Makes 1 × 250 ml bottle

12 cloves garlic
1 cup white vinegar

Peel garlic but leave cloves whole. Put them in a sterilised bottle with a close-fitting cork or non-metallic lid. Pour in vinegar. Stand in warm place for 2 weeks. Strain and discard the garlic. Rebottle in a sterile container and seal.

HERB VINEGAR

Makes 1 × 350 ml bottle

1½ cups white vinegar
3 sprigs single herb

Put the vinegar in a sterilised bottle. Add the sprigs of washed herb. Cover with a non-metallic lid. Stand in a warm, dry place for about 14 days before using. The herb may be left in vinegar while it is being used, or removed, according to preference.

MIXED HERB VINEGAR

Makes 2 × 300 ml bottles

---

1 tablespoon roughly chopped chives
1 tablespoon roughly chopped
  marjoram
1 tablespoon roughly chopped
  tarragon
1 tablespoon roughly chopped parsley
2⅓ cups white vinegar

Pack mixed herbs into sterilised bottles or jars. Add the vinegar. Cover and tightly seal the containers with non-metallic lids. Stand in a warm place for 4 weeks. Strain, pour into sterilised bottles and cork securely.

LEMON VINEGAR

Makes 2 × 250 ml bottles

---

1 lemon
2 cups white vinegar

With a potato peeler, thinly pare the yellow rind from the lemon, making sure no white pith is attached to it. Put half the rind into each of the sterilised bottles. Add the vinegar. Cover and tightly seal the bottles with non-metallic lids. Stand in a warm place for 2 weeks. Before use, if it is preferred, the vinegar may be strained and the lemon rind discarded.

MINT VINEGAR

Makes 2 × 300 ml bottles

2–3 good handfuls fresh mint leaves
2⅓ cups white vinegar

Strip the mint leaves from the stalks. Wash and pat the leaves dry. Pack the leaves in sterilised bottles or jars. Add the vinegar. Cover and tightly seal with non-metallic lids. Stand in a warm place for 3 weeks. Strain and pour into sterilised bottles. Cork securely.

MULBERRY VINEGAR

Makes 5 × 350 ml bottles

---

1 kg mulberries
7 cups white wine vinegar
sugar

Wash the fruit and put in a non-metallic bowl. Crush fruit and cover it with vinegar. Cover with a clean cloth and stand for 10 days, stirring daily. When ready to complete process, sterilise bottles and strain vinegar through a jelly bag. Measure liquid and put in pan. Add 200 g of sugar to each cup of liquid and stir over low heat to dissolve sugar. Boil for about 10 minutes. Skim, bottle and seal at once.

ONION VINEGAR

Makes 4 × 250 ml bottles

---

125 g onions
4 cups wine vinegar

Peel and finely chop the onions. Put in a clean, dry jar with the vinegar. Let stand for 2 weeks. Shake daily. After 2 weeks, sterilise bottles and strain vinegar. Pour into bottles and seal.

ORANGE VINEGAR

Makes 4 × 350 ml bottles

---

juice and rind of 6 oranges
6 cups wine vinegar
extra orange rind

Thinly pare the orange rind and put it in a pan with the vinegar and squeezed orange juice. Heat slowly to boiling point. Remove from heat and transfer to a large, non-metallic bowl. Cover and let stand for 2 weeks. When ready to continue, sterilise bottles and strain vinegar through a sieve. Pour into bottles. Put thin strip of fresh, washed rind in each bottle. Seal.

PICKLING VINEGARS

There are three methods for making pickling vinegars. The type of vinegar used will depend on personal preference and also whether white or brown pickles are being made. White wine and cider vinegar will give clear pickles, while malt vinegar and red wine vinegar will discolour the produce. Spiced vinegar may be made especially for a particular pickle. When using the first method, the vinegar must be boiled at some point during the pickling or chutney process, otherwise the product will not keep for long. If the vinegar is boiled, as in methods 2 and 3, it must be allowed to cool before the pickles are added.

METHOD 1
5 cups vinegar
2 tablespoons white peppercorns
2 tablespoons whole allspice
2 tablespoons cloves
4-cm piece cinnamon stick

Only whole spices can be used in this method. Put the vinegar in a large, sterilised jar and add the spices. Securely seal the container. Allow to stand for 1–2 months. Shake the jar at least once a week. Then strain off the spices, and bottle the vinegar in sterilised bottles. Seal well.

METHOD 2
5 cups vinegar
4 tablespoons whole pickling spices

Put the vinegar in a pan and add the spices. Cover and bring slowly to the boil. Remove from the heat. Allow to steep for 2–3 hours. Sterilise bottles, strain vinegar, bottle and seal.

METHOD 3
4 tablespoons whole pickling spices
5 cups vinegar

Sterilise the bottles. Tie the pickling spices in a muslin bag. Put in pan and add the vinegar. Bring slowly to the boil. Boil for 15 minutes. Remove the muslin bag. Pour into bottles and seal.

RASPBERRY VINEGAR

Makes 4 × 250 ml bottles

1 kg raspberries
2½ cups white vinegar
sugar

Wash the raspberries. Crush with a wooden spoon and put in jar or bowl with the vinegar. Cover and stand for 7 days, stirring several times a day. To complete, sterilise bottles. Strain vinegar through a jelly bag and measure liquid. Put in a pan with ⅓ cup of sugar to each cup of juice. Heat gently, stirring until the sugar is dissolved, then boil rapidly for 10 minutes. Bottle and seal *immediately*.

SHALLOT VINEGAR

Makes 2 × 300 ml bottles

---

50 g shallots
2½ cups white wine vinegar or 1¼ cups vinegar and 1¼ cups white wine

Peel and finely chop shallots. Put in an airtight, sterile bottle with vinegar and store for 2 weeks. Then strain and rebottle vinegar in sterilised bottles. Seal well.

STONE FRUIT VINEGAR

Makes 5 × 250 ml bottles

---

3 kg stone fruit (e.g. apricots, plums, cherries, damsons, greengages and peaches)
4 cups vinegar
sugar
brandy to taste (optional)

Choose good quality, well-ripened fruit. Halve the fruit, but do not remove the stones. Put the fruit in a bowl, and add the vinegar. Cover with a clean cloth and allow it to stand for 6 days. Once a day, stir and press the fruit with a wooden spoon. Finally, sterilise bottles, press the fruit again and drain off the liquid through a jelly bag. Measure the liquid and pour into a pan. Add 200 g of sugar to each cup of liquid and stir until dissolved. Then boil steadily for 15 minutes until the vinegar is syrupy. Stir in the brandy, if desired. Skim, bottle and seal immediately.

TARRAGON VINEGAR

Makes 2 × 300 ml bottles

2–3 good handfuls fresh young tarragon leaves
2⅓ cups white wine vinegar

Wash and dry the tarragon leaves. Lightly bruise them and place in sterilised bottles or jars, adding the vinegar. Cover. Leave to stand in a warm place for 3–4 weeks. Finally, sterilise the bottles. Strain the vinegar, bottle and cork well.

SPICED VINEGAR

Makes 6 × 350 ml bottles

---

9 cups vinegar
4 tablespoons peeled and chopped root ginger
4 tablespoons peppercorns
4 tablespoons salt
1¼ cups sugar
½ teaspoon cayenne pepper
1 tablespoon cloves
1 tablespoon whole pickling spices

Sterilise bottles. Put all the ingredients in a pan. Boil for 15 minutes, then remove from heat and allow to cool. Strain through double muslin. Pour into bottles. Cork securely.

PICKLES

Pickles are made from almost any kind of vegetable or fruit that is of good quality and not over-ripe. Pickles may be sweet, hot or tangy. The ingredients should be quite chunky, unlike chutney and relish where they are more finely chopped. Pickles are often left to stand overnight in a covered bowl. This does not have to be in the refrigerator – the kitchen bench is suitable.

It is most important to buy a good quality vinegar of at least 5 per cent acetic acid, as the pickles rely mainly on the preservative ability of this acid. As a general rule, the vinegar in pickles is left unthickened, though in some cases, as in mustard pickles, the thickening and flavouring is the feature. The flavour of malt vinegar blends well with pickles, though white vinegar is sometimes preferred if colour is important. Although wine vinegar has a delicate flavour, in most pickles and chutneys it is wasteful to use it. A good flavour is imparted by cider vinegar. Spicing the vinegar will improve the flavour of pickles. A wide variety of spices, some hot, some fragrant, can be used: type and quantity is a matter of personal taste.

The adding of sugar, and also the quantity used, is another personal choice. Avoid the use of brown sugar when a light vinegar is used, because of the colour. Some pickles are cooked in the vinegar, while others are not. The degree of crispness of the pickle is determined by the length of time that the ingredients are cooked.

As with other preserves, the cleaning and sterilisation of the jars, bottles, lids and corks, is very important. Again, the use of metal tops is unwise, as the acid in the vinegar will corrode the metal and give the pickle a most unpleasant taste. If the pickling vinegar is cold, the pickles do not need to be hot, so neither do the jars.

ARTICHOKE PICKLES

Makes 1 × 500 ml jar

---

250 g Jerusalem artichokes
1 onion
2 tablespoons salt
2 teaspoons mustard powder
½ teaspoon turmeric
2 cups cider vinegar
1 teaspoon mustard seeds
3 tablespoons sugar
½ teaspoon blade mace
½ teaspoon cloves

Wash, peel and cut artichokes into small chunks. Peel and slice onion. Put onion in one non-metallic bowl, and artichokes in another. Cover vegetables with water and put 1 tablespoon of salt in each bowl. Let stand overnight. Next day, sterilise the jar. Drain vegetables and rinse. Re-drain. Mix mustard powder and turmeric to a paste with a little of the vinegar. Put remaining vinegar in a medium-sized pan. Stir in the paste, mustard seeds, sugar, mace and cloves. Let simmer 5 minutes. Put artichokes and onions in the hot vinegar. Heat thoroughly but do not cook. Pack vegetables and spices in hot jar. Just cover with vinegar. Seal when cool.

DO NOT USE COPPER, IRON OR BRASS PANS WHEN MAKING CHUTNEYS, RELISHES, PICKLES AND SAUCES

SPICED BEETROOT PICKLES

Makes 1 × 500 ml jar

---

2 kg cooked beetroot
2⅓ cups vinegar
1 tablespoon salt
1 cup sugar
1 teaspoon peppercorns
1 teaspoon mustard seeds
1 teaspoon cloves
5-cm piece peeled root ginger

Sterilise the jar. Skin cooked beetroot. Cut into slices. Pack into dry jar. Put the vinegar, salt and sugar in a pan. Tie spices in a muslin bag and add to pan. Cover and simmer for 15 minutes. Discard the bag and pour the boiling vinegar over the beetroot in the jar. Seal.

BEETROOT AND HORSERADISH PICKLES

Makes 1 × 500 ml jar

---

1 kg small beetroot
4 teaspoons grated horseradish
2½ cups wine vinegar
⅓ cup sugar
1 teaspoon salt
1 teaspoon mustard powder
1 teaspoon whole pickling spices

Sterilise the jar. Cook, skin and dice beetroot. Put in hot jar with the grated horseradish. Put vinegar, sugar, salt and mustard in a pan. Tie the pickling spices in a muslin bag and add to pan. Bring to the boil and simmer for 15 minutes. Remove the muslin bag. Pour the boiling vinegar into the jar and seal.

CAULIFLOWER AND PINEAPPLE PICKLES

Makes 6 × 350 ml jars

1 large cauliflower
1 large green pepper
500 g onions
¼ cup salt
3 cups white vinegar
1 × 450 g can pineapple pieces
½ cup plain flour
1 cup sugar
1 tablespoon curry powder
2 tablespoons mustard powder

Wash and slice cauliflower. Deseed pepper and chop in thin strips. Slice onions. Put cauliflower, pepper and onion in non-metallic bowl, sprinkle with salt and let stand overnight. Next day, sterilise the jars, then drain and rinse vegetables. Put in pan with vinegar. Bring to boil and boil for 20 minutes. Drain pineapple, reserving juice. Add pineapple pieces to vegetables. Mix flour, sugar, curry powder and mustard to a smooth paste with the pineapple juice. Stir into pan and cook for about 5 minutes until mixture boils and thickens. Pack and seal.

CELERY PICKLES

Makes 4 × 350 ml jars

2 green peppers
2 red peppers
500 g celery
4 onions
2½ cups white vinegar
1 cup sugar
4 teaspoons salt
4 teaspoons mustard seeds
1 teaspoon turmeric
2 tablespoons cornflour
3 tablespoons water

Sterilise the jars. Deseed and thinly slice green peppers. Dice red peppers. Thinly slice celery and onions. Put vegetables in bowl. Cover with boiling water and stand for 10 minutes, then drain. Put vinegar, sugar, salt, mustard seeds and turmeric in pan. Bring to boil. Add vegetables. Boil, stirring, for 5 minutes. Blend cornflour and water together to a paste and add to vegetables in pan. Boil for a further 3 minutes. Pack into hot jars. Seal.

CHOKO PICKLES

Makes 6 × 350 ml jars

1.75 kg chokos
625 g onions
1 cup chopped green beans
1 cup chopped celery
5 tablespoons salt
1 cup sugar
5 cups malt vinegar
1 teaspoon turmeric
2 tablespoons mustard powder
1 tablespoon curry powder
½ cup plain flour
1 cup extra malt vinegar

Peel and deseed chokos. Cut chokos and onions into small pieces. Put in separate bowls. Put chopped beans and celery together in another bowl. Sprinkle salt over each bowl. Cover and let stand overnight. Next day, sterilise the jars, then drain vegetables and put in pan with the sugar, 5 cups of vinegar, turmeric, mustard and curry powders. Boil steadily for 20 minutes. Blend flour and extra vinegar together and stir into pan. Boil a further 5 minutes, stirring continuously. Pack and seal.

CHOKO AND CUCUMBER PICKLES

Makes 4 × 350 ml jars

---

2 large chokos
2 large cucumbers
2 large onions
2 red peppers
½ cup salt
3¼ cups white vinegar
2 cups sugar
2 teaspoons curry powder
1 teaspoon celery seeds
1 teaspoon mustard seeds

Peel and core chokos. Wash and deseed cucumbers. Peel onions. Halve and deseed peppers. Cut all into 2.5-cm cubes. Put in non-metallic bowl, sprinkle with salt and let stand overnight. Next day sterilise the jars, then drain vegetables and rinse. In a pan put vinegar, sugar, curry powder, celery seeds and mustard seeds. Stir over low heat until the sugar dissolves, then bring to boil. Add the vegetables. Bring back to boil. Reduce heat and simmer for 5 minutes. Pack and seal.

CHOKO MUSTARD PICKLES

Makes 3 × 350 ml jars

4 chokos
250 g onions
250 g celery
6 cups water
3 tablespoons salt
2 cups malt vinegar
½ cup sugar
½ teaspoon ground ginger
½ teaspoon curry powder
pinch of cayenne pepper
1½ teaspoons peppercorns
½ teaspoon cloves
2 tablespoons extra malt vinegar
2 teaspoons plain flour
1½ teaspoons mustard powder
1½ teaspoons turmeric

Peel, core and cut chokos into 2-cm cubes. Chop onions and celery. Put chokos, onions and celery in a non-metallic bowl with water and salt. Stand for 12 hours. Sterilise the jars. Drain and rinse vegetables. Put vegetables, the 2 cups of vinegar, sugar, ginger, curry powder and cayenne pepper in a pan. Tie peppercorns and cloves in a muslin bag and add to pan. Bring to boil and boil for 20 minutes. Mix the extra vinegar with the flour, the mustard and the turmeric and add to the pan. Continue to boil for 5 minutes or until the vegetables are just tender. Remove the bag of spices. Pack into hot jars and seal.

CLEAR MIXED PICKLES

Makes 2 × 500 ml jars

½ small cauliflower
250 g beans, sliced
12 shallots, peeled
1 cucumber, cubed
1 red pepper, sliced
5 tablespoons salt
spiced vinegar (see p. 117)

Divide cauliflower into small florets and put in a non-metallic bowl with the beans. In another non-metallic bowl put shallots and cucumber. Sprinkle each bowl with 2 tablespoons of salt. Put red pepper in a separate bowl with rest of salt. Stand all vegetables overnight. Next day sterilise the jars, then drain vegetables and rinse. Put cauliflower and beans in sieve and pour boiling water over them. Drain. Combine vegetables in jars. Cover with vinegar and seal.

DON'T FORGET TO LABEL AND DATE YOUR PRESERVES

DON'T USE METALLIC TOPS FOR SEALING ANY PRESERVE CONTAINING VINEGAR

STORE YOUR PRESERVES IN A COOL, AIRY, DRY, DARK PLACE

CUCUMBER AND PEPPER PICKLES

Makes 5 × 500 ml jars

6 large cucumbers
10 onions
6 green peppers
½ cup salt
4 cups sugar
2 cups vinegar
2 tablespoons celery salt
1 cup water
3 tablespoons whole pickling spices
½ cup curry powder

Peel and finely slice cucumbers and onions. Deseed and finely slice the peppers. Place all in a non-metallic bowl. Sprinkle with salt, and cover with water. Let stand overnight. Next day sterilise the jars, drain vegetables thoroughly and rinse. Add sugar, vinegar, celery salt, water, and pickling spices in a muslin bag. Boil for 10 minutes. Remove bag, add curry powder and remove from heat. Pack and seal.

CURRIED CUCUMBER PICKLES

Makes 7 × 350 ml jars

6 cucumbers
3 onions
3 peppers
½ cup salt
2 cups sugar
3¼ cups white vinegar
2 teaspoons curry powder
1 teaspoon celery seeds
1 teaspoon mustard seeds

Cut cucumbers and onions into 5-mm slices. Cut peppers into 1-cm pieces. Put all in a non-metallic bowl and sprinkle with the salt. Cover and stand for 5 hours. Drain well. Sterilise the jars. Put sugar, vinegar, curry powder, celery seeds and mustard seeds in a pan. Stir over low heat until the sugar dissolves. Bring to the boil. Add the drained vegetables and bring back to the boil. Pack into hot jars and seal.

SWEET CUCUMBER PICKLES

Makes 6 × 350 ml jars

500 g cucumber
500 g onions
500 g cauliflower
10 cups cold water
¾ cup salt
¾ cup plain flour
2 cups sugar
1 tablespoon mustard powder
1 tablespoon turmeric
½ teaspoon ground pepper
¾ cup extra water
2½ cups vinegar

Dice all the vegetables and put in non-metallic bowl. Make a brine with the 10 cups of water and salt. Pour over the vegetables. Leave to stand overnight. Next day sterilise the jars, then transfer the vegetables and brine to a pan and boil for 5 minutes. Drain. Mix the flour, sugar, mustard, turmeric and pepper to a smooth paste with the extra water. Add the vinegar. Put in a large pan and bring to the boil. Mix in the vegetables and boil for 5 minutes. Pack and seal.

> TO CHOP ONIONS, CUT THE SKINNED ONION IN HALF, THEN PLACE THE FLAT SIDE DOWN ON A BOARD AND HOLD THE STALK END WHILE SLICING ACROSS

FRUIT AND VEGETABLE PICKLES

Makes 8 × 350 ml jars

1 large beetroot
1 small cucumber
1 cooking apple
2 peaches
2 nectarines
1 kg ripe apricots
1 kg ripe tomatoes
2 large onions
6 green beans
5 cups vinegar
1 cup sugar
6 tablespoons plain flour
1 tablespoon turmeric
1 tablespoon curry powder
¼ cup extra vinegar

Sterilise the jars. Wash beetroot and partly cook it in boiling water. Peel and chop. Peel and cut up cucumber. Peel and stone or core fruit, except the tomatoes. Slice onions. Top and tail beans. Mince or finely chop all the fruit and vegetables, place in a pan and barely cover with the 5 cups of vinegar. Boil 15 minutes, stirring occasionally to prevent sticking to the pan. Add the sugar and stir until dissolved. Mix together flour, turmeric, curry powder and the extra vinegar. Stir into the boiling mixture, and continue to boil for 2 minutes. Pack into hot jars and seal.

MELON SWEET AND SOUR PICKLES

Makes 4 × 350 ml jars

1.75 kg honeydew melon
2 tablespoons salt
1¼ cups white vinegar
1 teaspoon whole pickling spices
a small piece peeled root ginger
3 cups sugar

Cut melon in strips, discarding skin and seeds. Put in sieve. Sprinkle with salt and stand for 2 hours. Sterilise the jars. Wash melon to remove salt and put in a pan. Add vinegar to pan, and the spices and ginger tied in a muslin bag. Bring to the boil and simmer for 5 minutes. Remove from heat and stand until cold. Add sugar. Heat slowly, stirring to dissolve sugar, then simmer for 5 minutes. Remove bag. Pack melon into hot jars. Pour the hot liquid over the melon. Seal.

MUSTARD PICKLES

Makes 5 × 350 ml jars

2 cups peeled and chopped cucumber
2 cups chopped onions
2 cups tiny cauliflower florets
2 cups sliced beans
¾ cup salt
5 cups water
2½ cups malt vinegar
½ cup plain flour
¾ cup sugar
2 teaspoons mustard powder
½ teaspoon celery seeds
1 teaspoon turmeric
¼ teaspoon paprika
pinch of cayenne pepper
½ cup extra water

Put prepared vegetables in a non-metallic bowl. Sprinkle with salt, cover with the 5 cups of water, cover bowl and stand for 24 hours. Next day, sterilise the jars. Strain vegetables, rinse well and set aside. Put vinegar in large pan. Blend flour, sugar, mustard, celery seeds, turmeric, paprika, pepper and ½ cup of water. Heat the vinegar to boiling and then stir in the flour and spice thickening. Continue stirring until mixture boils and thickens. Add drained vegetables. Heat until mixture returns to boiling. Pack in hot jars, cover until cool and seal.

PICCALILLI PICKLES

Makes 5 × 500 ml jars

---

500 g pickling onions
500 g marrow, peeled
125 g green beans
1 small cauliflower
250 g cooking apples
¾ cup salt
3 fresh chillies
3 cloves
30 g peeled root ginger
4 cups white vinegar
½ cup sugar
1 tablespoon cornflour
1 tablespoon turmeric
¼ cup mustard powder
2 tablespoons extra white vinegar

Cut the vegetables and apples into 2-cm pieces. Put on a large dish, sprinkle with salt and let stand overnight. Next day, sterilise the jars. Tie the chillies, cloves and ginger in a muslin bag. Put in pan with the 4 cups of vinegar. Simmer for 20 minutes, then remove the muslin bag. Add the vegetables and sugar to the pan and simmer for another 20 minutes. Mix the cornflour, turmeric and the mustard powder to a smooth paste with the extra vinegar. Add to the pan and stir until it is boiling. Boil for 3 minutes, stirring constantly. Pack into hot jars and seal.

RED CABBAGE AND ONION PICKLES

Makes 3 × 500 ml jars

---

750 g red cabbage
250 g pickling onions
¼ cup salt
a large piece peeled root ginger, crushed
6 black peppercorns
4 cloves
¼ teaspoon whole allspice
1 stick cinnamon
2 cups red wine vinegar
⅔ cup water
¼ cup sugar

Cut cabbage into quarters, remove core, shred and wash well. Slice into 1-cm shreds. Put in basin with onions and salt. Mix well. Let stand for 24 hours, stirring several times during the day. Next day, sterilise the jars, then rinse vegetables well and drain thoroughly. Pack into hot jars. Put the ginger and spices in a muslin bag and put in a pan with the vinegar, water and sugar. Bring to the boil and simmer for 15 minutes. Remove bag. Pour hot vinegar over cabbage. Seal.

DO NOT USE COPPER, IRON OR BRASS PANS WHEN MAKING CHUTNEYS, RELISHES, PICKLES AND SAUCES

SWEET AND SOUR PICKLES

Makes 4 × 350 ml jars

2 red peppers
1 green pepper
2 medium-sized cucumbers
6 small onions
2 small carrots
¼ cauliflower
¼ cup salt
2 cups white vinegar
2 cups sugar
2 teaspoons celery seeds
1 tablespoon mustard seeds
¼ teaspoon turmeric

Deseed peppers. Chop unpeeled cucumber, peppers and onions into 1-cm cubes. Peel and cut carrots into strips. Break up cauliflower. Put all the vegetables in a non-metallic bowl. Sprinkle the salt over the top and let stand overnight. Next day sterilise the jars, then drain and rinse the vegetables. In a large pan put vinegar, sugar, celery and mustard seeds and turmeric. Stir until sugar dissolves. Bring to boil. Add vegetables. Bring to boil again then immediately remove from heat. Pack the vegetables in hot jars and cover with vinegar liquid. Seal.

GREEN TOMATO PICKLES

Makes 4 × 500 ml jars

1 kg green tomatoes
500 g onions
¾ cup salt
7 cups water
2 green peppers
1 red pepper
5 cups cider vinegar
1½ cups brown sugar
pinch of cayenne pepper
1 tablespoon mustard powder
½ teaspoon ground mixed spice
½ teaspoon curry powder
¼ teaspoon ground ginger
¼ teaspoon ground cinnamon
1 teaspoon celery seeds
¼ cup extra water

Wash and slice tomatoes. Slice onions. Put both in a non-metallic bowl with salt and water. Let stand for 24 hours. Next day, sterilise the jars and drain vegetables. Wash, deseed and dice peppers. Heat vinegar and sugar to boiling point in a large pan. Stir in the peppers, tomatoes and onion. Mix cayenne pepper, mustard, mixed spice, curry powder, ground ginger, cinnamon and celery seeds to a paste with ¼ cup of water. Stir into the other ingredients. Cook slowly for about 45 minutes, stirring often, until tomatoes are clear. Pack into hot jars and seal.

TOMATO AND CHOKO PICKLES

Makes 4 × 350 ml jars

1 kg ripe tomatoes
1 kg chokos
2 onions
3 teaspoons salt
1 teaspoon mustard seeds
¼ teaspoon paprika
¼ teaspoon ground ginger
¼ teaspoon ground cinnamon
¼ teaspoon ground allspice
1¼ cups sugar
1 cup white vinegar

Sterilise the jars. Pour boiling water over tomatoes and let stand 30 seconds, then peel the skins off and chop the flesh roughly. Peel, core and chop chokos. Finely chop onions. Put the vegetables in a large pan with salt, mustard seeds, paprika, ground ginger, cinnamon and allspice. Stir over a low heat. Bring to the boil, then reduce heat and simmer, uncovered, until chokos are tender – about 1 hour. Stir sugar and vinegar in a small pan, uncovered, until sugar dissolves. Add to vegetables. Simmer gently over low heat for a further 30 minutes, until the mixture is thick. Pack while hot. Seal.

ZUCCHINI AND ONION PICKLES

Makes 2 × 350 ml jars

500 g small zucchini
125 g small pickling onions
2 cups white vinegar
1½ teaspoons salt
1½ teaspoons black peppercorns
1 tablespoon sugar
2 tablespoons cold water

Sterilise the jars. Cut zucchini into quarters, lengthwise. Peel onions. Put vinegar, salt, peppercorns, sugar and water in a pan. Bring to the boil and simmer for 5 minutes. Add zucchini and onion. Stir while bringing back to simmering point, then remove from heat. Pack the vegetables into hot jars and cover with the vinegar. Seal.

MUSTARDS

CURRY MUSTARD

Makes about 125 g

¼ cup white mustard seeds
2 teaspoons white peppercorns
1 teaspoon curry powder
¼ teaspoon turmeric
¼ cup oil
¼ cup malt vinegar
¼ cup red wine
1 teaspoon salt

Sterilise jars or pots. Place mustard seeds, peppercorns, curry powder and turmeric in blender and blend to a fine powder. Add the oil, vinegar, wine and salt and blend for a few seconds until all are combined. Spoon into jars or earthenware pots. Cover and leave for 24 hours before using.

GARLIC AND PARSLEY MUSTARD

Makes about 125 g

¼ cup white mustard seeds
2 teaspoons peppercorns
1 clove garlic
¼ cup oil
¼ cup vermouth
¼ cup white wine vinegar
1 teaspoon salt
2 tablespoons finely chopped parsley

Sterilise jars or pots. Place mustard seeds, peppercorns and garlic clove in the blender. Blend to a fine powder. Add the oil, vermouth, vinegar and salt. Blend for a few seconds until all are combined. Mix in parsley. Spoon into jars or earthenware pots. Cover and leave for 24 hours before using.

PAPRIKA MUSTARD

Makes about 125 g

¼ cup white mustard seeds
2 teaspoons white peppercorns
1 teaspoon paprika
¼ cup oil
½ cup white wine vinegar
1 teaspoon salt

Sterilise jars or pots. Place mustard seeds, peppercorns and paprika in the blender. Blend to a fine powder. Add the oil, vinegar and salt. Blend for a few seconds until all are combined. Spoon into jars or earthenware pots. Cover and leave for 24 hours before using.

RED WINE MUSTARD

Makes about 125 g

¼ cup white mustard seeds
2 teaspoons black peppercorns
¼ cup oil
¼ cup white wine vinegar
¼ cup red wine
1 teaspoon salt

Sterilise jars or pots. Place mustard seeds and peppercorns in the blender. Blend to a fine powder. Add the oil, vinegar, wine and salt. Blend for a few seconds until all are combined. Spoon into jars or earthenware pots. Cover and leave for 24 hours before using.

WHITE MUSTARD

Makes about 125 g

¼ cup white mustard seeds
2 teaspoons white peppercorns
¼ cup oil
½ cup white wine vinegar
1 teaspoon salt

Sterilise jars or pots. Place the mustard seeds and peppercorns in the blender. Blend to a fine powder. Add the oil, vinegar and salt and blend for a few seconds to mix with the mustard. Spoon into jars or earthenware pots. Cover and leave for 24 hours before using.

DON'T FORGET TO LABEL AND DATE YOUR PRESERVES

DON'T USE METALLIC TOPS FOR SEALING ANY PRESERVE CONTAINING VINEGAR

STORE YOUR PRESERVES IN A COOL, AIRY, DRY, DARK PLACE

SAUCES & KETCHUPS

Sauce is a term with a wide application in English, covering a variety of sweet and savoury liquids. Ketchup is an American term used to denote any piquant sauce containing vinegar. Sauces and ketchups are made from ingredients similar to chutneys. Vinegar is the preservative, and its proportion must be high enough to be effective. The fruit used for sauce must be ripe, but not over-ripe, or it may ferment or separate out, particularly if cooking time is too short. Sauces can be mild, sweet, tart, hot or fiery. If bright, well-coloured sauces and ketchups are desired the spices used should be tied up in a muslin bag, and then discarded.

Peeling fruit such as apples is not necessary, since the sauces are sieved or strained and then puréed. Passing the mixture through a colander or a coarse strainer results in a textured sauce containing small seeds. Finer sieves give a smoother sauce. A blender is effective, but if the mixture is processed for too long some seeds impart a bitterness. Do not use metal sieves or blenders with metal blades, as contact with the metal reduces the keeping quality of the sauce.

Sauces and ketchups should be bottled immediately after they have been puréed, while still hot, and will thicken as they cool. Bottles and stoppers must be sterilised before filling. Metallic tops must not be used, as the vinegar will react and cause corrosion. After the cork or the non-metallic top is put on, the bottle should be inverted, so that the air gap will be heated by the hot product – this will help the sauce to keep. Storing the sauce for several weeks before using will allow the flavour to develop.

APPLE AND TOMATO KETCHUP

Makes 2 × 350 ml bottles

---

350 g cooking apples
1.25 kg tomatoes
225 g onions
175 g brown sugar
1¾ cups spiced vinegar (see p. 117)
2 teaspoons dried marjoram
1 teaspoon paprika
2 cloves garlic

Sterlise the bottles. Wash apples. Chop roughly, including peels and cores. Put in a large pan with chopped tomatoes and onions. Add the sugar and other ingredients. Bring slowly to boil, stirring to dissolve sugar. Cover pan and boil for 1 hour, stirring occasionally. Let cool slightly and pass through sieve. Return to pan. Bring again to boil, then pack and seal.

HOT APPLE KETCHUP

Makes 2 × 350 ml bottles

---

1 kg cooking apples
450 g onions
4 green chillies
2⅓ cups vinegar
6 cloves garlic
175 g sugar
10 green cardamom seeds
2 teaspoons mustard seeds
2 teaspoons ground ginger

Sterlise the bottles. Wash the apples but do not peel. Chop up roughly. Chop onions and deseed and chop up the chillies. In a pan put the apples, onions and chillies together with the vinegar, chopped garlic, sugar, cardamom and mustard seeds and ground ginger. Mix together and bring to the boil. Cover the pan. Simmer the mixture for 45 minutes, stirring occasionally. Allow the mixture to cool slightly, then press through a fine sieve. Put the purée in a clean pan. Bring back to the boil. Immediately pack into the hot bottles and seal.

BOYSENBERRY SAUCE

Makes 4 × 250 ml bottles

1.5 kg boysenberries
1 orange
2 large cooking apples
1 large onion
1½ cups brown sugar
2 cups vinegar
1 teaspoon mustard powder
1 teaspoon ground cinnamon
1 teaspoon ground ginger
½ teaspoon ground cloves
½ teaspoon ground nutmeg
½ teaspoon salt

Sterilise the bottles. Put boysenberries in pan. Bring to boil and simmer until pulped. Press the pulp through a fine sieve and put in a pan. Thinly peel the orange and shred the rind finely. Remove and discard the white pith from the orange. Chop the orange flesh. Peel, core and finely chop the apples and onion and add to the pan. Add orange rind and flesh, and all other ingredients and stir to dissolve sugar. Bring the mixture to the boil. Simmer about 15 minutes, or until the mixture becomes thick, stirring occasionally. Pack in hot bottles and seal.

BLACKBERRY KETCHUP

Makes 4 × 250 ml bottles

1.5 kg blackberries
spiced vinegar (see p. 117), made
* with cider vinegar*
soft brown sugar

Sterlise the bottles. Wash blackberries. Put in pan without any water. Simmer over a low heat until soft. Rub through a sieve. Measure the purée. Put back in pan. For every 2 cups of fruit pulp, add 1 cup of spiced vinegar and 40 g of sugar to the pan. Stir to dissolve sugar, then simmer until thick, stirring often. Pack in hot bottles and seal.

CHILLI SAUCE

Makes 2 × 250 ml bottles

185 g mixed red and green chillies
125 g cooking apples
185 g onions, chopped
2/3 cup white vinegar
1 teaspoon salt
2 teaspoons prepared mustard

Sterilise the bottles. Remove stalks and seeds from the chillies. Chop very finely. Peel, core and chop up the apples. Put the chillies, apples,

onions, vinegar, salt and mustard in a pan. Heat gently, stirring until mixture boils. Simmer for about 40 minutes, until the vegetables and fruit are very soft and mushy and the mixture has thickened. Press through a sieve. Pack immediately into hot bottles and seal.

CRANBERRY SAUCE

Makes 2 × 350 ml bottles

500 g cranberries
2/3 cup white wine vinegar
250 g sugar
1/2 teaspoon salt
1 teaspoon ground mixed spice

Sterilise the bottles. Wash the cranberries. Put in a pan with the vinegar. Cook gently until the berries have softened and the skins have burst. Sieve fruit to remove skins and return to pan. Add the sugar, salt and spice. Continue cooking over a low heat, stirring, until the mixture thickens. Pack into hot bottles and seal.

CUCUMBER AND MINT SAUCE

Makes 2 × 350 ml bottles

1 kg cucumbers
2 tablespoons salt
2 cooking apples
1 onion
1 cup white vinegar
½ teaspoon extra salt
¼ cup sugar
1 teaspoon dill seeds
2 tablespoons chopped fresh mint

Peel the cucumbers. Cut lengthways into quarters and remove the seeds. Grate or finely chop the cucumber flesh. Place it in a nonmetallic bowl and sprinkle with the 2 tablespoons of salt. Cover and leave to stand overnight. Next day sterilise the bottles, then drain and rinse the cucumber under cold, running water. Peel the apples and the onion. Chop. Put the apples, onion, cucumber, vinegar, ½ teaspoon of salt, sugar, dill seeds and chopped mint into a pan. Simmer gently for about 1 hour, until pulpy. Stir occasionally. Press through a sieve or put through a blender to get a smooth sauce. Return to pan and reheat to boiling point, then pack into hot bottles and seal.

FRUIT SAUCE

Makes 5 × 250 ml bottles

1 kg ripe tomatoes
500 g cooking pears
500 g cooking apples
¾ cup currants
350 g onions, chopped
1¼ cups white vinegar
2 teaspoons mustard powder
¼ teaspoon cayenne pepper
2 teaspoons salt

Sterilise the bottles. Without peeling, cut up the tomatoes, pears and apples. Put in a pan with the currants and the onions. Simmer until the fruit is very soft – if the pears are hard, this may take up to 2 hours. Put through a sieve and return the pulp to the pan. Mix together the vinegar, mustard powder, cayenne pepper and salt and add to the pan. Bring to the boil. Boil for 3 minutes, or until sauce has thickened. Pour into hot bottles and seal.

DO NOT USE COPPER, IRON OR BRASS PANS WHEN MAKING CHUTNEYS, RELISHES, PICKLES AND SAUCES

DON'T USE METALLIC TOPS FOR SEALING ANY PRESERVE CONTAINING VINEGAR

STORE YOUR PRESERVES IN A COOL, AIRY, DRY, DARK PLACE

GOOSEBERRY KETCHUP

Makes 2 × 350 ml bottles

750 g gooseberries
500 g brown sugar
²/₃ cup vinegar
1 teaspoon ground cinnamon
1 teaspoon ground allspice
1 teaspoon ground cloves

Sterilise the bottles. Top and tail the gooseberries. Wash them thoroughly and put in a pan. Add the sugar, vinegar, cinnamon, allspice and cloves. Stir well together. Bring slowly to the simmering point while stirring. Cook over a gentle heat for 1½–2 hours, stirring the mixture often. Pour into hot bottles and seal.

GUAVA SAUCE

Makes 1 × 350 ml bottle

1.5 kg guavas
1¼ cups vinegar
1½ teaspoons salt
½ cup sugar
½ teaspoon ground cloves
½ teaspoon ground cinnamon
½ teaspoon ground allspice

Sterilise the bottles. Wash guavas. Put in pan. Add vinegar and salt. Boil for 20 minutes. Remove from heat. Pass through a sieve to remove the seeds. Put the strained mixture in a pan. Add the sugar, cloves, cinnamon and allspice. Stir to dissolve the sugar. Boil for 45 minutes, stirring occasionally. Pack into hot bottles and seal.

KIWIFRUIT SAUCE

Makes 2 × 350 ml bottles

1 kg kiwifruit
6 cloves
3 cloves garlic
12 peppercorns
1-cm piece peeled root ginger
12 whole allspice
1½ cups sugar
1½ cups white vinegar
pinch of cayenne pepper
1 teaspoon salt

Sterilise the bottles. Peel and roughly slice kiwifruit. Put in a pan. Tie the cloves, garlic, peppercorns, chopped root ginger and allspice in a muslin bag. Add to pan, together with the sugar, vinegar, cayenne pepper and salt. Bring to the boil, stirring to dissolve sugar. Boil for about 30 minutes, or until soft and pulpy. Remove the spice bag and discard. Press the mixture through a sieve, or put through a blender. Put the purée in a clean pan. Bring back to the boil. Immediately pack into hot bottles and seal.

MUSHROOM KETCHUP

Makes 1 × 350 ml bottle

350 g mushrooms
100 g brown sugar
300 ml vinegar
1 onion, finely chopped
1 tablespoon ground allspice
1 tablespoon salt
pinch of black pepper

Sterilise the bottle. Cut mushrooms in quarters. Put in a pan with other ingredients. Bring to the boil, stirring to dissolve sugar. Cover the pan. Simmer for 30 minutes. Cool slightly. Process until smooth in a blender. Return to cleaned pan. Bring back to boil, pack in hot bottle and seal.

PLUM SAUCE

Makes 4 × 250 ml bottles

1 kg plums
2 fresh red chillies
175 g onions, sliced
2½ cups spiced vinegar (see p. 117)
1 tablespoon salt
1 teaspoon whole allspice
2-cm piece peeled root ginger
1 teaspoon ground cinnamon
½ cup sugar

Sterilise the bottles. Stone and chop the plums. Seed and chop the chillies. Put plums, chillies, onions, half the vinegar, and salt in pan. Tie the allspice and root ginger in a muslin bag. Add to pan. Simmer for about 30 minutes, or until the fruit is very soft. Remove bag. Sieve. Return to pan. Add cinnamon, sugar and rest of vinegar. Stir until the sugar has dissolved. Simmer for about 1 hour or until the mixture has thickened. Pack into hot bottles and seal.

RED PLUM SAUCE

Makes 4 × 250 ml bottles

1 kg red plums
4 cups white wine vinegar
2 cups brown sugar
¾ cup sultanas
3 cloves garlic, crushed
1 teaspoon cayenne pepper
1 tablespoon salt
1 tablespoon mustard seeds

Sterilise the bottles. Halve and stone the plums. Put all the ingredients together in a pan, stirring over low heat to dissolve sugar. Cover pan and simmer for about 1 hour, or until the fruit is very soft. Strain through a sieve. Pack into hot bottles and seal.

AVOID USING OVER-RIPE
FRUIT, DAMAGED OR BRUISED
PIECES OF FRUIT, OR ANY
DISEASED FRUIT

SIMPLE TOMATO KETCHUP

Makes 2 × 350 ml bottles

450 g onions
1.5 kg ripe tomatoes
175 g sugar
⅔ cup red wine vinegar
3 cloves garlic, crushed
1 teaspoon salt
3 tablespoons mustard powder

Sterilise the bottles. Roughly chop up the onions and the tomatoes. Mix them together in a pan. Add all other ingredients. Bring the mixture to the boil. Simmer about 45 minutes, stirring occasionally. Do not cover the pan. Allow to cool slightly. Purée in a blender. Then press the purée through a sieve. Return to a clean pan. Bring to the boil. Remove from heat and immediately pack into hot bottles and seal.

TOMATO SAUCE

Makes 5 × 350 ml bottles

4 kg tomatoes
4 large onions
8 cloves garlic
½ teaspoon cayenne pepper
1½ teaspoons peppercorns
1½ teaspoons whole allspice
12 cloves
5½ cups vinegar
1½ cups sugar
2 teaspoons salt

Sterilise the bottles. Chop up the tomatoes. Peel and roughly chop onions and garlic. Put all vegetables in the pan with the cayenne pepper. Tie peppercorns, allspice and cloves in a muslin bag. Add to the pan. Cook for about 30 minutes until vegetables are tender. Discard bag of spices. Put mixture through a blender and return to pan. Add vinegar, sugar and salt. Boil gently for 1 hour, stirring occasionally. Pack in hot bottles and seal.

SPICY TOMATO SAUCE

Makes 3 × 350 ml bottles

4 tomatoes
3 onions
3 cooking apples
2 red peppers
1 green pepper
1 cup vinegar
½ cup sugar
½ cup raisins
1 tablespoon salt
½ teaspoon pepper
½ teaspoon ground ginger
½ teaspoon ground cinnamon
¼ teaspoon ground nutmeg
¼ teaspoon ground cloves

Sterilise the bottles. Peel the tomatoes, onions and apples. Remove the seeds from the peppers. Roughly chop all the vegetables. In a pan put the vinegar, sugar, raisins, salt, pepper and spices. Bring to the boil, and add all the chopped vegetables. Simmer, uncovered, for 1 hour, stirring occasionally. Remove from heat and put through a blender. Return to clean pan. Bring back to boiling point, then pack into hot bottles and seal.

TOMATO AND PEPPER SAUCE

Makes 2 × 300 ml bottles

1.5 kg ripe tomatoes
500 g onions
375 g green peppers
2 cups chilli vinegar (see p. 112)
2 teaspoons salt
½ teaspoon mustard seeds
½ teaspoon ground cloves
½ teaspoon ground allspice
½ cup sugar

Sterilise the bottles. Chop up the tomatoes and vegetables and put in a pan with vinegar, salt and spices. Bring slowly to the boil. Simmer for about 30 minutes or until the tomatoes and vegetables are very soft. Put through a sieve. Return to the pan and add the sugar, stirring until the sugar has dissolved. Simmer for about 1 hour, or until the mixture thickens. Pack into hot bottles and seal.

FRUIT & NUT BUTTERS

Butters are generally made from a mixture of puréed fruit and sugar, blended and cooked until a spreadable paste-like preserve is obtained. They require constant attention while cooking, as the mixture will curdle if it is boiled. They can be stored for up to 1 month in a cool, dark place, and up to 3 months in a refrigerator. They make a welcome change from jam and jelly.

APPLE BUTTER

Makes 3 × 300 ml jars

8–9 medium-sized apples (e.g.
  Golden Delicious)
1 teaspoon water
1 orange
450 g light brown sugar

Sterilise the jars. Wash apples. Quarter and core. Place in a pan with the water, cover, and simmer on low for 30 minutes until soft. Grate the rind of the orange and reserve. Squeeze the juice into the grated rind. Press the cooked apples through a sieve. Discard the skins. Return the pulp to the pan and stir in the sugar, grated rind and juice. Simmer over very low heat, stirring frequently, for about 1½ hours or until thick. Remove from heat and ladle into jars, leaving 1-cm gap at the top, and seal immediately.

To help prevent the apple butter from separating, pour about 6 cm of hot water into the cleaned pan and bring to the boil. Place the jars of apple in the pan and cover. Boil for 10 minutes. Allow to cool before storing.

APRICOT BUTTER

Makes 2 × 200 ml jars

100 g dried apricots
½ cup water
65 g unsalted butter
4 tablespoons sugar
juice of 1 lemon
1 large egg, lightly beaten

Soak the apricots overnight in a non-metallic bowl. Drain and discard the water. Next day, sterilise the jars. Put the apricots and ½ cup of clean water in a pan and stir until boiling. Reduce the heat and simmer until all the water is absorbed and the fruit is mushy. Transfer to a food processor and purée. Melt the butter over hot water in a double saucepan, add the sugar and lemon juice. Cook, stirring, for 2 minutes. Add the beaten egg while still stirring, then add the puréed fruit. Remove from heat and pour into warm jars. Cover and seal. When cool, store in a cool, dry place.

DON'T FORGET TO LABEL AND
DATE YOUR PRESERVES

STORE YOUR PRESERVES IN A
COOL, AIRY, DRY, DARK PLACE

AVOID USING OVER-RIPE
FRUIT, DAMAGED OR BRUISED
PIECES OF FRUIT, OR ANY
DISEASED FRUIT

BANANA AND PASSIONFRUIT BUTTER

Makes 3 × 175 ml jars

---

2 lemons
175 g butter
¾ cup white sugar
pinch of salt
2 egg yolks
½ cup passionfruit pulp
2 bananas, mashed

Sterilise the jars. Squeeze the lemons. In the top part of a double saucepan put the butter, lemon juice, sugar, salt and egg yolks. Add the passionfruit pulp and the mashed bananas. Place the pot over simmering water. Stir the mixture until the back of a wooden spoon becomes thickly coated. Remove from heat and pour into hot jars. Cover and allow to cool. When cool, seal and store in a cool, dry place.

CASHEW BUTTER

Makes 2 × 230 ml jars

---

2 cups raw cashew nuts
6 tablespoons oil
salt

Sterilise the jars. Preheat oven to 180°C. Spread a single layer of cashew nuts on a flat, ovenproof plate. Pour oil over them. Put in the oven and roast until cashews are golden brown – about 15–20 minutes. From time to time, toss them with a fork. Remove from the oven and allow them to cool. Roast any remaining cashews in the same way. Put about ½ cup of roasted cashews in a blender. Blend until the paste is as smooth as desired. Add salt to taste. Add more oil, if necessary, to form a more spreadable paste. Repeat until all cashews are blended. Pack into small jars. Cover, seal and store in the refrigerator.

FIG BUTTER

Makes 3 × 250 ml jars

---

370 g dried figs, without stems
1 cup orange juice
1 cup water
1 small lemon, chopped (rind intact)
½ cup brown sugar

Sterilise the jars. Put the figs, orange juice, water and the chopped lemon in a pan and bring to boiling point. Reduce the heat and simmer until the fruit is tender. Remove from heat and allow to cool. Process in blender until it is smooth. Replace in the pan and stir in the sugar. Over a low heat stir the mixture until it is thick enough to spread. Spoon into warm jars, cover, seal and store in a cool place.

GINGER AND LEMON BUTTER

Makes 2 × 250 ml jars

6 egg yolks, beaten
¾ cup castor sugar
1 teaspoon grated lemon rind
1 cup lemon juice
¼ cup preserved ginger, finely
   chopped
1½ teaspoons ground ginger
180 g unsalted butter

Sterilise the jars. In the top half of a double saucepan put the egg yolks and sugar. Stir until well mixed. Stir in lemon rind and juice, the gingers, and the butter, in small pieces. Over simmering water, stir the mixture until it will thickly coat the back of a wooden spoon. Remove from the heat and pour into hot jars. Cover, and seal when cool. Store in a cool, dry place.

LEMON BUTTER

Makes 3 × 250 ml jars

4 eggs, lightly beaten
¾ cup sugar
½ cup lemon juice
¼ cup water
125 g unsalted butter
2 teaspoons grated lemon rind

Sterilise the jars. Put the beaten eggs and sugar in the top of a double saucepan. Stir until mixed well. Gradually add the lemon juice and water, stirring until they are combined. Roughly chop the butter and add with the lemon rind. Put the pan over simmering water, and stir the mixture until it thickly coats a wooden spoon. Pour into hot jars. Cover the jars and seal. Store in a cool, dry place.

LEMON AND LIME BUTTER

Makes 3 × 250 ml jars

180 g butter, chopped
2 cups castor sugar
½ cup lemon juice
1 teaspoon grated lime rind
⅓ cup lime juice
4 eggs, beaten and strained

First sterilise the jars. In the top half of a double saucepan put all the ingredients, and stir until they combine. Place over simmering water. Stir until the mixture thickly coats a wooden spoon. Pour into hot jars, cover and allow to cool. When cold, seal and store in a cool, dry place.

LEMON AND PASSIONFRUIT BUTTER

Makes 3 × 250 ml jars

12 passionfruit
2 teaspoons grated lemon rind
4 eggs, beaten and strained
¾ cup castor sugar
½ cup lemon juice
125 g butter, chopped

Sterilise the jars. Cut passionfruit in halves and scoop out the pulp. Put all ingredients in the top half of a double saucepan. Place over simmering water and stir until the mixture thickly coats a wooden spoon. Pour into hot jars, cover and allow to cool. When cold, seal and store in a cool, dry place.

ORANGE BUTTER

Makes 3 × 250 ml jars

250 g white sugar cubes
3–4 oranges
125 g unsalted butter
5 eggs, beaten and strained

Sterilise the jars. Rub the sugar cubes over the rind of the oranges until they have absorbed the colour and the zest. Squeeze the oranges to get ¾ cup of juice. Melt the butter slowly in a pan, then stir in the juice and sugar. Gently heat until the sugar dissolves. Stir 1 tablespoon of the hot mixture into the beaten egg, repeating this until all is combined. Put the mixture in the top half of double saucepan and stir it over simmering water until a wooden spoon becomes thickly coated. Remove from heat and pour into hot jars. Cover and let cool. When cold, seal and store.

ORANGE AND PASSIONFRUIT BUTTER

Makes 3 × 250 ml jars

2 passionfruit
5 eggs, beaten and strained
¾ cup castor sugar
3 teaspoons grated orange rind
½ cup orange juice
125 g butter, chopped
¼ cup water

Sterilise the jars. Cut the passionfruit into halves and scoop out the pulp. Place the beaten eggs and sugar in the top half of a double saucepan. Stir in the passionfruit pulp and add the other ingredients. Stir the mixture over simmering water, until the back of a wooden spoon becomes thickly coated with mixture. Remove from heat and pour into hot jars. Cover and let cool. When cold, seal and store.

> AVOID USING JARS THAT ARE NOT PERFECT. THEY MAY BREAK WHEN A HOT PRESERVE IS POURED INTO THEM

PEANUT BUTTER

Makes 2 × 230 ml jars

---

2 cups raw peanuts
6 tablespoons oil
salt

Sterilise the jars. Preheat oven to
180°C. Spread a single layer of
peanuts on a flat, ovenproof plate.
Drizzle oil over them. Put the peanuts in the oven and roast for
about 20 minutes until they are
lightly browned. Toss occasionally
with a fork. Remove from the oven
and allow them to cool. Leave the
skins on. Roast any remaining peanuts in the same way. Put ½ cup
of peanuts into a blender. Blend
until as smooth as desired. Add
more oil, if necessary, to obtain a
more spreadable paste. Add salt to
taste. Repeat until all peanuts are
blended. Pack in small jars. Cover,
seal and store in the refrigerator.

PLUM BUTTER

Makes 3 × 350 ml jars

---

500 g red plums
¼ cup lemon juice
4 eggs, beaten and strained
¾ cup castor sugar
125 g butter, chopped

Sterilise the jars. Remove the stones
from the plums and roughly cut up
the flesh. Place in a saucepan with
the lemon juice. Bring to the boil,
cover and simmer until the plums
are soft – about 20 minutes.
Remove from the heat. Put sieve
over a bowl and push plum mixture
through. Discard the pulp in the
sieve. In the top half of a double
saucepan stir the eggs and sugar
until mixed. Stir in the plum mixture and the butter. Stir the mixture
over simmering water until the back
of a wooden spoon becomes thickly
coated. Remove from heat and
pour into hot jars. Cover and allow
to cool. When cold, seal and store
in a cool, dry place.

CRYSTALLISED FRUITS

Crystallised fruits and peels need to be thoroughly dried, but not over-dried, as this would make the preserve hard. Syrup in which they are cooked must be syrupy but not toffee-like.

CRYSTALLISED ANGELICA

desired number of young angelica
  stalks
2 tablespoons salt
2 cups boiling water
2 cups sugar
2 cups water
extra sugar

Use proper angelica, not the shiny-leaved ornamental angelica, which has very little flavour, and select young stalks. Wash them well and cut in 8-cm lengths. Put in a non-metallic bowl. Dissolve the salt in the boiling water. Pour over the angelica, cover and stand for 24 hours.

Remove the angelica from the water and remove any strings. Wash the flesh. Boil together the 2 cups of sugar and water for 10 minutes. Into this put the angelica and simmer for 15 minutes. Lift the angelica out and put it on a plate. Reserve the sugar syrup.

Next day reboil the angelica in the syrup. Repeat this on the third day. Lift out the angelica and allow it to drain until there are no more drips. Sprinkle some of the extra sugar on a plate and lay the angelica on it. Sprinkle on more sugar. Put the plate of sugar and angelica in an airing cupboard or very cool oven and let dry for several days. Store in an airtight jar.

CRYSTALLISED APRICOTS

1 × 850 g can apricot halves
sugar

Drain the apricots, reserving the juice. Measure the juice, pour into a saucepan and add ½ cup of sugar to each cup of juice. Over a moderate heat dissolve the sugar, then bring the syrup to the boil and boil steadily for 3 minutes. Do not stir. Add the fruit and simmer gently for 3 minutes. Remove from heat. Allow the fruit to stand overnight in the syrup.

Repeat the boiling and standing for a further 2 days. Lift apricots on to a tray lined with greaseproof paper. Dry off in a very cool oven (about 100°C) for a few hours. Remove apricots from paper and roll in sugar. Store in airtight jars.

CRYSTALLISED ORANGE PEEL

2 oranges
½ cup sugar
½ cup water
extra sugar

Cut the oranges into quarters. Cut out the flesh with a sharp knife and discard. Cut peel into strips 5 mm wide. Cover with water and bring to the boil. Remove from heat and drain well. Repeat this boiling process 6 times and then drain well.

Into a saucepan that is large enough to take the peel, but small enough that the syrup will not boil away, put the sugar and water. Bring to the boil and simmer for 5 minutes. Stir to dissolve the sugar. Put the peel into the gently boiling water and continue to cook until the syrup is absorbed by the peel. Do not stir, but move the peel about gently so all the pieces can be in syrup.

Sprinkle some of the extra sugar on a flat plate. Lift peel from the pan and put in a single layer on the plate of sugar. Sprinkle more sugar over it. Leave to dry for several days, and turn the peel occasionally, sprinkling more sugar over it as necessary. When dry, store in an airtight jar. The same process may be used for other peels.

CRYSTALLISED PINEAPPLE

1 × 450 g can pineapple rings
sugar

Drain the pineapple. Measure the juice and pour into a large saucepan. Add 1 cup of sugar to each cup of the juice. Over a moderate heat, stir until the sugar has dissolved. Bring to boil. Boil steadily, without stirring, for 3 minutes. Add the drained pineapple and simmer gently for 3 minutes. Remove from the heat and allow to stand overnight.

Next day, bring the fruit and syrup to the boil and simmer gently again for 3 minutes. Remove from heat and let stand overnight again. Repeat this for another 2 days.

Line a tray with greaseproof paper. Lift the fruit from the syrup with a draining spoon and put it in a layer on the tray. Place the tray of pineapple in a very cool oven (about 100°C) for a few hours. Lift from the paper and store in airtight jars.

CRYSTALLISED VIOLETS

violets
egg white
castor sugar

Pick the violets. Immerse in water and shake them to loosen the dirt and free them of insects. Remove from the water and lay to dry on a clean tea towel.

Remove the stems and as much as possible of the green at the base of the flowers. Have ready a dish of lightly beaten egg white and another of castor sugar. Brush each violet lightly and evenly over the egg white. Carefully dip it in the castor sugar, then shake off the excess.

Place the violets in a single layer on an oven tray. Dry them off in a very cool oven (about 100°C) for a few hours. Remove the violets from the tray and store in an airtight container.

FRUIT LIQUEURS

Fruit liqueurs are made by steeping fruit, sometimes mixed with other ingredients, in spirits. The fruit flavours the liquid, and sugar is added to sweeten. The best spirits to use are brandy, gin, vodka or white rum. If stewing improves the flavour of the fruit it is cooked in wine rather than water and sugar is added at the cooking stage. Fresh or frozen berries give equally good results for a berry liqueur.

Liqueurs must always be sealed tightly to avoid evaporation and must be stored in a cool, dark place. They should stand for at least 6 weeks after bottling before being used. Cherry brandy, and liqueurs that are mixed with the fruit and left standing for a period before bottling, are excepted.

To infuse, leave the bottle or jar of fruit and spirit in a warm place, stirring occasionally until the sugar is dissolved and the desired flavour is achieved. Strain and pour into sterilised bottles. Seal securely with sterilised corks.

APRICOT LIQUEUR

Makes about 1.75 litres

---

1 kg apricots
2½ cups white wine
1 cup sugar
1 teaspoon whole allspice
2½ cups brandy

Sterilise a bottle or jar large enough to take all ingredients. Cut the apricots into halves and remove the stones. Put the apricots and the wine in a large saucepan and bring to the boil. Simmer until the fruit is soft. Remove from heat and mash. Add the sugar and allspice. Return to the heat. Stir, without boiling, until the sugar dissolves. Bring to the boil, cover, and simmer for 5 minutes. Remove from the heat and pour into a large sterilised bottle or jar. Leave in a warm place for 4 or 5 days. Strain, squeezing out all the juice. Add the brandy. Sterilise bottles and pour liqueur into them. Seal with sterilised corks. Store in a cool, dark place.

APRICOT STONE LIQUEUR

Makes about 875 ml

---

stones of 500 g apricots
1 cup sugar
2½ cups brandy

Wash and thoroughly dry the apricot stones. Crush them with a mal-let or heavy rolling pin. Put the crushed stones in a sterilised jar with the sugar and brandy. Cover tightly. Shake well. Put aside in a warm place for about 4 weeks. Stir or shake occasionally. Strain through muslin cloth and pour into sterilised bottles. Seal tightly with sterilised corks. Store in a cool, dark place.

BLACKBERRY LIQUEUR

Makes about 1 litre

---

1 kg blackberries
1 kg sugar
2 cups water
1 teaspoon ground nutmeg
3 cups brandy
1 cup vodka

Sterilise the bottles. Wash berries. Allow to dry. Put the berries in a large saucepan with the sugar, water and nutmeg. Over heat, without boiling, stir until sugar is all dissolved. Bring to the boil and simmer, uncovered, for 30 minutes or until it is reduced by about three-quarters. Strain through muslin cloth. Reserve the liquid and discard pulp. Pour into a jug and add the brandy and the vodka. Pour into sterilised bottles. Seal tightly with sterilised corks. Store in a cool, dark place.

BLACKCURRANT LIQUEUR

Makes about 875 ml

500 g blackcurrants, topped and
  tailed
3.5-cm piece cinnamon stick
2–3 cloves
2½ cups brandy
1½ cups sugar

Sterilise a large bottle or jar to take all ingredients. Put the blackcurrants in a bowl and mash them with a potato masher. Put the mashed fruit in the bottle with the spices. Add the brandy and sugar. Cover tightly and leave in a warm place for 4–8 weeks. Strain through muslin cloth, squeezing out as much liquid as possible. Pour into sterilised bottles. Seal tightly with sterilised corks. Store in a cool, dark place.

CHERRY BRANDY LIQUEUR

Makes about 1 litre

500 g stoned cherries
1 cup sugar
3 cups brandy
1 cinnamon stick

Prick cherries with a fork. Put in a sterilised jar large enough to take all ingredients. Add the sugar. Cover with a tight-fitting lid. Let stand for 2–3 days. Shake the jar

from time to time to help the juice to appear. Add the brandy and cinnamon to the contents of the jar. Seal up the jar again tightly. Allow to stand for 3 months in a cool, dark place. Shake from time to time. Unseal and strain through muslin cloth. Reserve the liquid and discard pulp. Pour the liquid into sterilised jars or bottles. Seal tightly with sterilised corks. Store in a cool, dark place.

CHERRY STONE LIQUEUR

Makes 2 × 250 ml bottles

stones of 500 g cherries
2½ cups brandy
1 cup sugar

Wash and thoroughly dry the cherry stones. Crush them with a mallet or a heavy rolling pin. Put in a sterilised jar with the brandy. Add the sugar. Cover and shake well. Leave in a warm place for 4 weeks. Shake from time to time to dissolve the sugar. Strain through muslin cloth. Pour into sterilised bottles. Seal with sterilised corks. Store in a cool, dark place.

DON'T FORGET TO LABEL AND
DATE YOUR PRESERVES

STORE YOUR PRESERVES IN A
COOL, AIRY, DRY, DARK PLACE

COFFEE BEAN LIQUEUR

Makes about 875 ml

---

9 mocha coffee beans
2½ cups white rum
1 cup sugar

Put the coffee beans in a sterilised bottle or jar and pour in the rum. Cover tightly and leave in a warm place for about 8 weeks. Add the sugar, shake well, recover, and leave until the sugar dissolves. Strain through muslin cloth. Pour into sterilised bottles. Seal with sterilised corks. Store in a cool, dark place.

FRUIT SALAD RUM LIQUEUR

---

200 g each seasonal fruit (e.g. gooseberries, strawberries, cherries, plums, currants, apricots, peaches, apples, pears, pineapple, mandarins)
sugar
dark rum

Fruit salad rum liqueur is a very special concoction that is not cheap to make. The fruit in it can be eaten as an exotic dessert with cream, ice-cream or on its own. As many or as few different fruits may be used as desired, and layers of different fruit can be built up over weeks. The flavoured rum makes a lovely drink, or it can be used as a flavouring in another dish.

Thoroughly clean a large container with a lid. This container should be opaque, for light will spoil the colour of the fruit. The fruit must be ripe, but in perfect condition. It must be washed and well dried. Small fruits are left whole, but larger ones are peeled, cored and cut into sections.

Allow 200 g of each fruit, and for each portion of fruit allow 100 g of sugar and sufficient rum to cover to a depth of 1 cm. Put first fruit in container, add sugar and sufficient rum to just cover. Cover with lid and store. Repeat this operation with each fruit as it comes into season. Keep the container covered, except when adding to the contents. Allow liqueur to stand for about 2 to 4 weeks before sampling, to allow the full flavour of the fruit to penetrate the liquid.

ORANGE LIQUEUR

Makes about 875 ml

---

36 sugar cubes
3 large Seville oranges
2½ cups white rum

Rub the cubes of sugar against the oranges until they are a deep orange colour and have absorbed the zest. Peel the oranges, removing the white pith and discarding it and the pips. Cut up the flesh, put it in a sterilised bottle with the sugar and the rum. Cover tightly, shake, and put it in a warm place for 3 to 5 days. Uncover, strain through muslin cloth, and pour into clean, sterilised bottles. Seal with sterilised corks. Store in a cool, dark place.

ORANGE LIQUEUR WITH BRANDY

Makes about 500 ml

---

3 large Seville oranges
1¼ cups sugar
1 cup brandy
¼ teaspoon ground coriander
¼ teaspoon ground cinnamon

Using vegetable peeler, thinly peel the rind from the oranges and chop it up finely. Squeeze juice from the oranges until you have 1 cup. In a bowl put the orange juice, rind, sugar, brandy, coriander and cinnamon and mix together. Put into a sterilised jar and cover tightly. Let stand for 2 days. Stir occasionally. Uncover and strain through muslin cloth. Reserve the liquid and discard pulp. Pour liquid into clean, sterilised bottles. Seal with sterilised corks. Store in cool, dark place.

ORANGE LIQUEUR WITH CALVADOS

Makes about 750 ml

---

3 large Seville oranges
1 cinnamon stick
3 cups Calvados
1½ cups castor sugar

Using vegetable peeler, thinly peel the rind from the oranges and cut it into thin strips. In a bowl put the rind, cinnamon and Calvados and cover securely. Put bowl in refrigerator for 1 week. Then strain the liquid into another bowl through muslin cloth and discard the cinnamon and rind. Add the sugar to the liquid in the bowl and stir it until dissolved. Pour liquid into clean, sterilised bottles. Seal with sterilised corks. Store in cool, dark place.

PEACH AND ORANGE LIQUEUR

Makes about 500 ml

---

500 g peaches, washed, halved and
* stoned*
6-cm piece orange rind
1 cinnamon stick
¼ cup white sugar
1 cup brandy
¼ cup Cointreau

Chop the peaches up roughly. Put in a large bowl with the rind, cinnamon, sugar, brandy and liqueur. Cover tightly. Place in refrigerator for 1 week. Then strain the mixture into another bowl through muslin cloth. Pour liquid into clean, sterilised bottles. Seal with sterilised corks. Store in cool, dark place.

PEAR LIQUEUR

Makes about 1.25 litres

---

1 cup water
3 cups sugar
1 kg pears
2 cups vodka

Sterilise the bottles. Put the water in a large saucepan. Add the sugar. Heat without boiling and stir until the sugar dissolves. Peel, core and slice the pears. Add to the pan and bring to the boil. Cover and simmer for about 15 minutes, until the pears become transparent. Pour the contents of the saucepan into a bowl, cover, and allow the pears and the syrup to cool to room temperature. Through muslin cloth strain the liquid into another bowl. Pour vodka into the strained liquid. Pour into bottles. Seal with sterilised corks. Store in a cool, dark place.

PLUM LIQUEUR

Makes about 875 ml

---

500 g plums
2 cups sugar
2½ cups gin

Prick the plums well. Put plums and sugar in a sterilised jar large enough to take all ingredients. Cover tightly and let stand for 2 to 3 days. Add the gin and cover tightly. Put in warm place for about 8 weeks. Then strain the liquid through muslin cloth into a large bowl. Pour into clean, sterilised bottles. Seal with sterilised corks. Store in a cool, dark place.

STRAWBERRY LIQUEUR

Makes about 875 ml

---

500 g strawberries
2 cups gin
1 tablespoon grenadine syrup
¾ cup castor sugar

Hull the strawberries and chop them up roughly. In a large bowl put the strawberries, gin and grenadine and cover securely. Put in refrigerator for 2 days. Uncover the bowl and add the sugar. Cover with a clean cloth and allow to stand for about 2 hours, stirring from time to time to dissolve the sugar. Strain through muslin cloth into a large jug or bowl. Pour liquid into clean, sterilised bottles. Seal with sterilised corks. Store in a cool, dark place.

INDEX